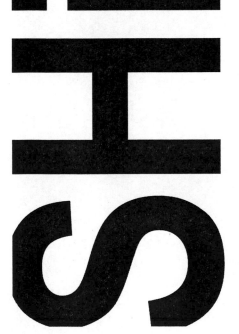

SHIFT

YOUR
MIND
SHIFT
THE
WORLD

SHIFT

YOUR
MIND
SHIFT
THE
WORLD

STEVE
CHANDLER

REVISED EDITION

MAURICE BASSETT
books for athletes of the mind

Shift Your Mind Shift The World

Maurice Bassett
P.O. Box 839
Anna Maria, FL 34216

Contact the publisher:
MauriceBassett@gmail.com
www.MauriceBassett.com

Contact the author:
www.SteveChandler.com

Editing by Kathryn McCormick
Editorial assistance and layout by Chris Nelson
Cover design by Carrie Brito

ISBN: 978-1-60025-128-3

Library of Congress Control Number: 2018909060

Revised Edition

To Maurice Bassett

One new perception,
one fresh thought,
one act of surrender,
one change of heart,
one leap of faith,
can change your life
forever.

~ **Robert Holden**

Table of Contents

Acknowledgments

To Kathy Eimers Chandler for editing and ground control. To Steve Hardison for the ultimate in coaching. To Byron Katie for the love, the work and the turnarounds. To Maurice Bassett, for being Director of the ACS and publisher extraordinaire. To Fred Knipe for delivering Dr. Ludiker and the wonderful singer-songwriter album, *9Ninety9*.

To my M6 colleagues Devon Bandison, Tina Quinn, Karen Davis, Kamin Samuel, Carolyn Freyer-Jones, Sherry Welsh, Melissa Ford and Gary Mahler.

To Darlene Brady for balancing and transcribing. To Frank Smith for playing "Better Than Anything" on Valentine's Day. To Marcus for the singing lessons.

To Dicken Bettinger for the Healing the World experience, to Michael Neill for everything he writes and the great Supercoach Academy, to Mark Howard for teaching me to listen and to Ankush Jain for allowing me to collaborate in his London class.

And to the beloved memory of Ed Eimers:

"Grandpa Ed Forever."

In a different state of mind, all of life looks different. Universally, all human beings stumble on that fact as their mind shifts into a different space.

~ Mara Gleason
One Thought Changes Everything

1

Dream small?

I used to think one had to dream big to achieve something great. My inner motivator would yell, "Buckle up, loser, we're going outside your comfort zone!"

I used to believe that was necessary. I believed people when they said that nothing great was ever created inside your comfort zone! So now I need to strap on my parachute and get ready to scare myself to death!

My personal growth heroes all seemed to say this. At least that's how I was hearing it. Dream big! Take the leap!

Until a light bulb got turned on in my mind: you could also dream small. That would work too.

Dream small? That was a game-changing mind shift.

Great things are done
by a series of small things
brought together.

~ **Vincent van Gogh**

2

Who died?

My niece once wore a tee shirt that said, "Who died and made you Elvis?"

Elvis! After my father, Elvis was my first true hero. Elvis Presley! King of rock and roll. He must have dreamed big, don't you think? Given his achievements in the world of entertainment, and his legendary status. I was sure he dreamed big all the way.

Look at what he achieved! The title of his second album of gold records was *50,000,000 Elvis Fans Can't Be Wrong.*

Feeding my assumption that he dreamed big was his movie called *Follow That Dream,* in which he sang, "You've gotta follow that dream wherever that dream may lead."

I assumed he meant follow that *big* dream.

But when I study the Presley biographies and interviews I find out that there was never a big dream. Never. In fact, it seemed like Elvis only dreamed small. (He wanted to be a truck driver.)

And what was his musical dream? To make a recording for his mother. That was it. Not to sing for millions of fans, but just for his mother.

This dream would cost him four dollars. That's how small it was. He paid his four dollars and went into a recording booth in Memphis and sang one song to give to his mother. After they recorded him they made him an acetate that he could put on his mother's turntable and play for her. A dream come true. (As small dreams always seem to do.)

But there was something about that recording that had the recording studio owner listen again and again. Something about that voice. Such an unusual combination of vulnerability and strength. There was innocence in it, but underneath there was swagger too. The owner would play it for people and say, "Believe it or not, this guy's white."

Months went by and Elvis was invited back into the studio to see what else he could do. He tried some more soft ballads with a couple of musicians, and it was okay but not amazing. Then during a break they started fooling around with an up-tempo rhythm and Elvis sang a wild and rocking version of "That's All Right Mama" and the studio owner came out of his chair.

The rest is history. And yet . . . no big dream was ever involved. Just a willingness to sing from the heart. And though his initial dream was small, his fame became huge.

And his story is just one of many that show us that even though big dreams are great and exciting, they're not necessary. You can go the other way too. You can *shift your mind* down to the smallest imaginable intention.

And the reason this is worth realizing is that so many people I have met become confused and feel inadequate when they can't come up with some kind of big dream to commit to and follow.

Wouldn't it be good for them to know that it's not always necessary?

You may have a fresh start
any moment you choose,
for this thing that we call "failure"
is not the falling down,
but the staying down.

~ Mary Pickford

3

Opportunity is already here

I used to wait around and hope somebody would give me a *big* opportunity. I used to think that was what I needed . . . a fresh start . . . so that I could show what I could do!

When you are like I was, chronically dissatisfied with life and unhappy with yourself, you often think something BIG has to happen OUT THERE IN THE WORLD to turn an inner feeling around.

I know I did.

So I tried hard to dream big. I didn't know this was an inner game, and that the perceived world wasn't going to "shift" without my awareness shifting first. I didn't know that.

I also didn't know that I could be happy with what I had. That happiness didn't have anything to do with exceptional achievement. Instead, I thought I probably had to be some form of a rock star like Elvis for this inner unhappiness to change.

And here's the irony: not even Elvis needed that. A major part of Elvis' appeal to the world was the joyful energy he was *already demonstrating* when he sang, even at the very start. People felt that.

The joy came first, not later after some kind of achievement or recognition.

Recently I found an old quote by Elvis in *Esquire* magazine in which he said, "All my life, I've always had a nice time. We never had any money or nothin', but we never were hungry, you know. That's something to be thankful for."

All his life he always had a nice time? Not just after he got rich and famous?

For most of my life my thoughts and beliefs kept me from having that kind of nice time. Those were not good days for me. Those were the days before the mind shifts started . . . those were the days when I thought thoughts like these:

"If only someone believed in me."

"When someone gives me the right opportunity, then I'll be on my way to being happy!"

"When I luck into the proper career that's my true calling, then I'll be able to display my true talent—the real me."

Then one day it shifted to this: *You can come from happiness right now.* You can have it be in every encounter. You can light up even the smallest task with enthusiastic creativity if you want to. That's the whole meaning of shifting in the mind. It happens in a heartbeat.

Just like shifting gears in a sports car. The shift doesn't take time. It's a roll of the wrist.

You are to create. Not to compete
for what is already created.

~ Wallace D. Wattles

4

Small starts acquire power and magic

Whatever it is, begin it. Just begin. Start creating. Don't think about doing the whole thing. You don't have to do the whole thing. You *never* have to do the whole thing at once.

In fact, you can't. So . . . just do the next thing.

Most people don't begin their project because they are always thinking about and picturing *the whole thing*. The very thought of the whole project is overwhelming, and soon they decide that they can't do this now. It's just too much.

"I'll have to wait till there's a lot of space in my life . . . or a lot more time . . . after certain other projects get done. Or at least until my energy rises."

My friend Scott, who used to be a bit chubby and out of shape, made a decision one day to do just twelve minutes of aerobic exercise each day. He just began. There. Whew, there's twelve minutes, over and done with.

Now he's been doing that minimum workout ever since. It's been many months, and he looks just great! Twelve minutes? Yes.

My friend Jim just sent me the following email, "Finally, I attended the national Attention Deficit Disorder Association's conference. I've been tested for ADD and have shown up as fitting the profile for 'inattentive ADD.' One giant piece of information I can share with you from the nation's leading researcher on the implications of exercise and brain function (John Ratey) is that **even 10 minutes** of exercise has major benefits for brain function (ability to focus, memory, etc.)."

Ten minutes is easy to think about. A long-term exercise program is harder to think about. Big thinking about major issues is often where procrastination comes from.

This is too big to do now.

I spent years and years pining away in cowardice for a shot at being a fiction writer. I always wanted that, but here I was with many decades having passed and still I had not begun. One day something told me, "Don't finish. Just begin."

It felt like a mind shift.

So I called my friend Sam Beckford and he and I started brainstorming the plot for a short business novel called *The Small Business Millionaire*. Of all the books I have ever written, it is my very favorite.

Then my mind seized up again. Could I now write a mystery novel that had nothing to do with business? The answer was no. I couldn't sit down and write a whole mystery novel! But then I saw that no one can. Who can do a whole thing at once?

What I could do, though, was begin.

So one day I just began. I put some words down. I did some research. I found out about a little lake in Michigan called Corpse Pond, and I was off and running. Could I write a mystery novel? Who knew? Who cared? But I knew I could begin. I ended up writing *The Woman Who Attracted Money.* A total joy.

So much of the advertising noise in our society encourages us *not* to begin . . . it encourages us to hang back and seek safety. Most products and services advertised day and night are designed to make us more comfortable and less challenged.

We'll help you back off from activity!

But challenge causes movement. Challenge will test our

skills and make us better. Challenge and the boldness to engage the challenge will transform us. Every challenge we face is an opportunity to create a more skillful, enthusiastic self.

And what is the best way to have fun with a challenge? We don't make it huge. We just begin. We begin something. It can be small.

If I never begin these things, then I'm living my life, in the image of the prize-winning poet William Olsen, like a flower "living under the wind."

I want to rise up into the wind. The wind is good for plants and trees and people like me. It blows strength into them. A motionless tree getting brittle in the windless sun in Arizona will snap apart in the first monsoon.

Same thing happens to a motionless me.

Something to try: pick a project. Then shift out of thoughts about doing the whole thing. Shift into simply beginning. Shift from visualizing future hours spent on something to spending just a few minutes getting it started. This shifts you into the present moment (the only place where great things are created).

What's called for on the Earth at this time is really a change of heart . . . the question is really not the future of humanity, but the presence of eternity.

~ Jack Kornfield

5

You can be a rebel with a cause

Let's say I am just learning how to drive, and I'm driving a sports car and James Dean is sitting next to me and I'm down there in second gear and the car's engine is kind of whining and complaining because I won't shift—I don't know how to shift!

How embarrassing. My one time to be with James Dean and look at me! Ever have a dream like this? And James is saying, "Just shift . . . please, it's time to shift" because James knows the engine is over-stressed and the car can only go so far in this gear, and you need to shift right now.

And that poor car just shakes and whines.

And that was my life.

Because I didn't know the mind can shift.

I wasn't alone. Most people just don't know. If they've never driven a sports car, they don't know what shifting really is and how easy it is for the spiral motion to set us free.

But if you *have* driven a stick-shift kind of car, you know that when you shift, the car starts to glide into a new level of speed. It now flows along the road and your feeling is freer with every shift.

And after a while, when you're in that next gear too long, it feels a little stressed again, it can't hold where the car wants to go, so it's time to shift again.

Well, your mind, your soul, your heart, your life, your brain, your whole complex picture is the same way . . . waiting for the shift inside the mind to allow the spiral release to occur.

The shift.

When you allow a shift in your mind, the world shifts with you.

When I coach people who are stuck somewhere (and a lot of different fearful thoughts hold them down in "stuck"), I know that what's next for them is a shift—a movement of that spiritual gear—a kind of gliding spiral, and the wrist is metaphorical—it's the mind—and it's an opening, and it's made of light. You open up . . . the thought ("I'm stuck!") drops away.

When the mind is open, it will shift.

When that happens all of life becomes, momentarily, light as a feather. Light as the breeze. Beautiful! You spiral up to the next level of consciousness: and . . . creativity, energy, vibration—whatever you want, you've got it. You can feel it, because you're gliding now.

Not powering. Not forcing. Not pushing. Not "crushing it." Just gliding. Allowing glide to happen.

The spiral is a spiritualized circle.
In the spiral form, the circle,
uncoiled, unwound,
has ceased to be vicious;
it has been set free.

~ Vladimir Nabokov
Speak, Memory

6

The biggest lie you've ever told

The best shifts in the mind are the shifts that take us from a lie to the truth.

In all my years of coaching, training and consulting, the most self-limiting lie people tell themselves is this one: "I'm not creative."

The self-image of not being creative throws a dark cloud of limitation over your day. Because deep down you suspect that creativity is the answer.

But with this belief called "not creative" in your head you are blindfolded and handcuffed in the face of a challenge. Life happens *to* you, not *with* you or *for* you.

Do you recognize that feeling of never quite finding the answer? You're walking through your day and you don't seem to have the answer to anything. Things get more problematic as you go.

This creativity lie has stopped everything. It has stopped you from being playful. It has stopped you from being mindful. It has made you a wallflower at the dance of your own life. Soon your world seems to consist entirely of living up to other people's expectations.

My friend Sandra was a consultant when she told me she was having trouble with a client of hers who wanted to hire her for a certain project. She didn't know what to decide to do—

what fee to charge, or what scope of work he expected.

I asked, "What do you want to create?"

She was startled by that question. Because Sandra didn't see herself as creative. So the word itself felt uncomfortable. She was just a person *trying to get by* and not have life be so difficult. But that was the whole problem. Her life was stuck on *difficult* because she was not creating.

When you know you can create, you can come back to your true, infinite self. Your life is now a canvas, and the pallet of paints is in your hands.

That's what I suggested that Sandra do. "Keep asking yourself what it is that *you* would like to create. You'll begin to feel your own energy and imagination as the primary force. It's no longer secondary. When you are creating you are composing the words and music to the whole show, just like your happiest moments as a child."

Sandra told me how much she loved creating things as a child. She made clothes and painted in watercolors and wrote poems to her grandparents. She could identify with the easy creativity of childhood. Even today she liked nothing better than being with children and talking to children. It reminded her of her own childhood.

But now Sandra was taken aback by my questions about her own creativity because for years and years she had forgotten *creation* as an option for herself. In her mind she had dropped creativity as her very source. She, like most adults, had learned to merely be defensive when it came to life. Life was something she was up against.

Notice that most people are like Sandra. They are like a football team would be that only played defense and never played offence. They could never design plays. So they could never run plays.

They would punt the ball away on first down.

A mind shift occurs when people think to cultivate, through a gentle practice of reflection, a self-awareness of being connected—at the depth of their being—to infinite creativity. It's a kind of self-awareness most people only associate with poets, artists and musicians. But it will work for everyone. It will work for you.

What do you want to create?

If the sun and moon should ever doubt,
they'd immediately go out.

~ William Blake

7

Doubt and the light goes out

Many people on the road to success are stopped by a moment of doubt . . . they doubt themselves. They don't have self-confidence. They don't trust themselves. They don't really believe in themselves.

I was working with a client the other day who had created a wonderful new product, a new service for people, and he was building a website for it, and he was getting very excited because he could see that once this was launched and the whole world could get access to it, he might be able to leave the job he was working on and really get into this full time!

Then, all of a sudden, he got really scared.

Is this really happening for me? Is it really true? Am I really worthy? Do I really deserve this?

All of us have had those moments. I know I have. But the point I want to remember is that my thoughts in those moments *do not serve me* on the road to success. They stop me.

There's a way out of those moments. Because those doubtful moments can't happen unless I'm focused on myself—unless I am starting to obsess about *me*, my fears, my welfare and my own survival.

The cure is to turn that around. Turn the whole focus around. Turn the spotlight toward the people my work will serve. Get it off of me!

Now I want to focus on the end user of my service. It's a surefire way out of self-doubt. It's a way out of fear—to focus on the client.

Think about the person out there in life who is *longing* to receive your service; someone who would really benefit from your ebook, or from some other product of yours. Someone who would really love it if you communicated with them and gave them what you had. Keep your focus on *them*, because that will get you back into action. That will have you less self-conscious about how you're coming across. Now you're trying to help. You want to contribute to their lives.

When you have information that would really help someone, you don't care how you say it or how you're coming across. You just want them to know about it. Shift the mind out to other people. Shift it off your self-conscious self.

Happiness is a simple everyday miracle,
like water, and we are not aware of it.

~ Nikos Kazantzakis

8

Yes, turn that spotlight on the crowd

I was once a guest lecturer teaching students the art of public speaking, and it wasn't long before their self-consciousness began to arise as an issue. As it always does when it comes to public speaking.

My students were graduate students with a wealth of skills and knowledge and beautiful things to bring to the world; but some were nervous about public speaking, and worried about getting up in front of groups to talk.

And this was despite the fact that what they had to talk about was powerful and inherently appealing. A fact they agreed with.

One student said, "I agree if people could get what I had to teach them it would really help them, but I'm scared that I'm not a good presenter, and I'm worried that I'm not a very good speaker, so I have these fears and doubts that kick in. I wonder, who wants to hear from *me*? Who am I really? Who wants to hear what I have to say?"

This fear isn't hard to understand. We grow up having these feelings pounded into us. My parents would say, "*Who are you to talk to a grownup that way?!?!*" Then we pound the thoughts and feelings into ourselves to even greater degrees as we get older.

Again I have found that the way out of this extreme

self-consciousness is to take the focus off of me. If I'm going to stand in front of a group of people and I have something that would really help them to hear or to learn about, I want to keep my focus on *them*. How can I help them? How can I serve them? How can I really light up their lives?

I don't care how I come across in this. I've got something for them, and it's my job to deliver it, and all I want to think about is them—what they need, what they would be helped by. Then I'll no longer be scared. It will take the focus off me. I can only be scared when I am focused on myself. I can't be scared while helping someone.

That's why you hear about people who wake up, look out the window, see the house across the street is on fire, run out of the front door, hear a little kid crying inside, then break through the burning wood, walk through the flames and pick up the child and run out.

Later people say, "Wow, what a courageous act! How did you find the courage in you?"

"It was never about me."

Picture someone who is in the desert dying of thirst, and here you come and you have water! You have a bottle of cold water and they're dying of thirst.

Are you worried about how you're dressed? What they might think of your hair? Or how to say the right thing when you walk up to them? Or whether you're a person someone would want water from?

Come on, man, they're *dying*.

So therefore there's no focus on you. You allow your mind to shift over to them. So you have no fear. Because fear comes from self-focus. Protecting the ego.

Your job is to never worry about what people think of you. Or to doubt your compassionate self. Your only job is to bring the water.

Listen to what you know
instead of what you fear.

~ Richard Bach

9

Conflicts, depression and recession

My friend, marketing consultant and coach Scott Young, brought a Harley Davidson ad from a newspaper to our coaching school, and we pinned it to the wall.

Our school was the precursor and a major inspiration for a large mastermind of people that was later to be called *Club Fearless*. The ad's headline said it all: "WE DON'T DO FEAR."

It also said this: "Over the last 105 years in the saddle, we've seen wars, conflicts, depression, recession, resistance, and revolutions. We've watched a thousand hand-wringing pundits disappear in our rear view mirror. But every time this country has come out stronger than before . . . If 105 years have proved one thing, it's that fear sucks and it doesn't last long."

And down below on the page next to the Harley Davidson logo it said, "So screw it. Let's ride."

Indeed.

That's just exactly the mind shift we are looking for. Because it is true: fear does not last long. Once you're actually out on the road and riding.

Nothing or nobody can make you
feel something you don't think.
Your thinking, and only your thinking,
creates your feelings.

~ Garret Kramer

10

Stories can put you in a prison

Some people *think* they don't get out on the road because they're lazy. They think they don't write, paint, make music, build bird houses, design homes, etc., etc., because they are lazy.

But laziness is just a story. We like to make stories up like this . . . stories about what we are like.

But soon they become chains. All of them.

Because the real fun is in the *action*—not the story. The real fun happens once you are up and riding. Therefore the story is, in fact, the very thing that keeps you off the bike.

But anyone can rise above a story. Or below it. Or beyond it. It's a mind shift. Anyone can leave any personal quality like "laziness" in the dust. Laziness will eat your dust. Shift the mind and the world shifts, too. Always both. Always simultaneous.

Q: What makes us spin all these stories?

A: We get fascinated with ourselves.

We become intoxicated just thinking about ourselves. Then we share with others what we think we are like. All the qualities we think we have, negative or positive, it soon doesn't matter. Lots of people even *brag* about being lazy.

"I was just too lazy to do that! I'm soooo lazy, ha ha ha ha ha. I *was* going to do that, but I was too lazy. I'm also too lazy to work out. I'm too lazy to learn a foreign language, so I'm going to take an interpreter with me when I go to that country. I know, I've been appointed ambassador, and it probably would be more professional of me if I learned the language of the country I was going to be in, but I'll have interpreters all around me, so let's just do it that way. I'm lazy. But you knew that. You knew that, didn't you? Have I told you about myself? Pull up a chair."

It's amazing how many American ambassadors refuse to learn the language of the country they are in. They say things like "I'm not good with languages," but to themselves or to their family they'll say, "I'm just too lazy to learn it. I admit it! I've always been lazy. Goes way back. All the way back. As a fetus I was lazy. Ha ha ha ha ha ha ha."

All these "lazy" personality traits we adopt are merely facets of fear. Because when we are in joyful and pure action, or joyful and pure relaxation, there is no fixed personality anymore. Certainly no laziness.

Buckminster Fuller used to say, "I seem to be a verb."

Maybe you were *not* too lazy to do that one thing in your life you always wanted to do. Maybe you were *afraid of something.*

But once you can see that, your mind is open. And the mind that is open will always shift.

Empty your mind. Be formless. Shapeless. Like water. Now you put water into a cup, it becomes the cup. You put water into a bottle, it becomes the bottle. You put it in a teapot, it becomes the teapot. Water can flow, or it can crash. Be water, my friend.

~ Bruce Lee

11

How do I set myself free?

Truth is beauty, and beauty sets you free.

Beautiful movement, like that of a dancer or an athlete, can be where your awareness of freedom comes from. It can also come from venturing forth. Going places I didn't know I could go.

Happiness is not some kind of pleasure I get eating chocolate bunnies or binge-watching vampire shows. That is really not happiness. That may feel like short-term pleasure. But it is often used to get myself out of my personal thinking and story-telling. Temporarily.

Spinning and then believing a story of laziness is a way of lying low instead of rising up. So when I'm "too lazy" to make my calls, I'm lying low instead of rising up. I am hanging back, instead of venturing forth. That's what my laziness story really is. It's a pause button. It's a retreat into passivity. It's a retreat into the seeming illusion, the false illusion (illusions are false by definition, aren't they?) that hanging back or lying low is SAFER for me than venturing forth.

So you see a person on the couch, and rather than being out this Saturday, going to his son's game, helping his neighbors, cleaning the yard, painting the bird house, taking a long walk—doing wonderful things, active things, the person is instead on the couch vegging out; and we say he's lazy, but really, deep down, he wants to hang back rather than venture forth. For safety's sake.

On the other hand the great dance teacher Martha Graham said, "I am a dancer. I believe that we learn by practice. Whether it means to learn to dance by practicing dancing or to learn to live by practicing living, the principles are the same."

Most people would never practice living. Ever. They are too busy trying to please others to enact and practice a vision of their own . . . not realizing that the very thing they might practice, like a Martha Graham ballet, or a Steph Curry jump shot, becomes the most pleasing thing in the world for others to behold.

I dwell in possibility.

~ Emily Dickinson

12

"You" die each time you shift

Art is eternal. Art saves lives. Picasso said that all children are born artists. He said, "The trick is to *remain* an artist." Throughout life. Throughout the dance of life.

"At times," Martha Graham said, "I hear the phrase 'the dance of life.' It is an expression that touches me deeply, for the instrument through which the dance speaks is also the instrument through which life is lived—the human body. It is the instrument by which all the primaries of life are made manifest. It holds in its memory all matters of life and death and love."

And it was designed for movement! That's why Nabokov took so many walks with his butterfly net in hand, and wrote standing up at his lectern! The body! And that's why the management guru Tom Peters' philosophy of "managing by walking around" is so effective. When managers get up from their desks and walk all around they can finally understand what's really going on. Through the factory, through the cubicles, here and there, stopping to shake hands (movement) and talk and walk on. We can do what Peters recommends. We can walk around.

Walk on, walk on, with hope in our hearts.

"Dancing appears glamorous, easy, delightful," says Martha Graham. "But the path to the paradise of the achievement is not easier than any other. There is fatigue so great that the body cries, even in its sleep. There are times of complete frustration, there are daily small deaths. Then I need all the comfort that practice has stored in my memory, a tenacity of faith."

Daily small deaths. How beautiful that is. Die a few times before you die.

I don't just want to call myself lazy and not understand the fear beneath it. I want to see it for what it is. Then I might just replace it with action.

You can replace any fear with action. Replace it. Throw the story out, get into action. Throw out the story of how unsafe this would be and get into action. Throw the story out first, and get into action, and laziness goes away. The shift is on.

My son in his bed in the morning was not lazy; he was afraid.

So the cure was to encourage him, somehow, usually by example—not by a lecture. Encourage. (Show him his innate courage!)

Same with my employees. They are not too lazy to cold call— they are afraid. So I want to encourage. When you encourage someone, you help them find the courage that's already there, so they can use it. Laziness is not a factor here. Fear is the only factor. Until the shift. Because all fear lives in the mind. It's never out there in the scary world.

If the only thing people learned
was not to be afraid of their experience,
that alone would change the world.

~ **Sydney Banks**

13

Try living your full life today

Did you know that the popular actor Paul Newman played the piano? I didn't either, until I saw him on Inside the Actors' Studio, and at the end of his interview, he wandered over to the piano and began playing.

Apropos of nothing.

He also made salad dressing. Newman's Own! And raced cars. And gave a ton of money to charity, and devoted lots of time to good causes, and stayed married to his wife all those decades, and was such a beautiful expression of the life force! Everything he did he put his carefree heart into. He didn't become over-identified with his story, his fame, or movies or anything else. He just lived.

Becoming over-identified with anything is to smother and mask the life force.

Like the actor Diahann Carrol is doing in her autobiography, *The Legs Are The Last To Go,* with a picture of her on the cover of the book over-identifying with her long legs. As if there were any way we ourselves could care any less about how her legs looked. This is a grotesque age of juvenile narcissism. Especially from adults. There's an exaggerated, neurotic focus on what other people think of how we look. Extreme and gross dependence on the approval of others.

Why not spend some time alone?

Solitude is where character, creativity and courage can grow strong. Where the shift happens. Yes, you want to be in the room where it happens.

"The honest truth is that it's sad to be over sixty," concludes Nora Ephron in her book, *I Feel Bad About My Neck.* If I were over-identified with the body, it *would* be sad to be over sixty. But how narcissistically juvenile am I willing to be? How emotionally underdeveloped?

So much so that I buy things I can't afford? Or that my eating is nothing more than an addiction that I pass off to myself as pleasure and emotional release? (I'm not condemning; I'm looking at my past life and identifying!)

I can allow a shift beyond this limited and limiting thinking. I can see this life turn around. Let all shifts begin with me.

I live in that solitude which is painful
in youth, but delicious in the
years of maturity.

~ Albert Einstein

14

Becoming healthy is such a shock

A reader of my blog wrote to me, "I would love to hear your take on our collective economy. Any ideas on how to be with this individually? Individually and collectively. I am aware of the paradox here. Any ideas?"

Yes. Always ideas. That's the joy of a shifting mind. It stirs up ideas like butterflies rising from a wind-blown bush. The mind can shift up from worries to ideas.

Here's one idea. Things are changing dramatically. Corrupt political systems are getting cleaned out so that we can build back stronger. Men in powerful positions who thought it was one of their "perks" to sexually abuse women are being called out and thrown out of their jobs.

It scares some people when longstanding institutions become healthy this fast. Hold on! Let me languish awhile. Let's not change so quickly. Let me pause for a moment or two longer to savor the false sense of wealth and power I used to have.

But change is a good thing. Can't you see? It allows us to develop collaboration and friendship in an age of narcissistic isolation. No longer do we have to ride the latest business bubble, or look for parental organizations to care for us. We grow.

Don't we?

It's certainly an available response to the times.

To rise up!

No matter what has ever happened in history, there were always heroic, creative responses to it by individuals who rose up. People like Anne Frank, Joan of Arc and Ayn Rand who stood up to tyranny with art and power. People like Viktor Frankl who rose up from the concentration camps with a beaming new psychological masterpiece. Frankl had written his psychological masterpiece prior to being thrown into the camps and the guards took it away and *burned* it. He re-wrote the whole book in his mind! That was the one thing they could not take away.

However, it is not always our first impulse to rise up and answer the challenge of changing times. As Andrew Cohen has said, "It seems to be the human tendency to want to resist change, to want to create the illusion of security in an insecure universe, and to avoid at all costs facing into the awesome and unlimited nature of life itself."

Life! Awesome and unlimited. (Easy for me to forget!)

Hard times can allow us to see that we ourselves share this awesome and unlimited nature.

I once started a club to teach people how not to join clubs. Club Paradox. How not to want to cling to authority too much when times are scary. How not to follow others. How to return to what's strong inside. Collaborative but independent! A club for individuals who are willing to learn Emersonian self-reliance and become artful and fearless. A club for people who want to express their awesome and unlimited natures without waiting for permission or coaching to do so.

Then I thought I'd keep writing books about the magic of the human spirit. Books about how creative we all are. Those are just some ideas. Your ideas will be even better. The smaller the better. The mind shifts. Worries are replaced by ideas.

And then the world itself shifts.

Every burned book or
house enlightens the world;
every suppressed or expunged
word reverberates through
the earth from side to side.

~ **Ralph Waldo Emerson**

15

The last thing we remember to do

Natalie Goldberg's priceless advice to writers is something all of us can use, whether we are writers or not.

Her advice was, "Keep your hands moving."

That's all! That's it! That's usually the last thing we think to do!

Doing things really isn't the problem. *Thinking about* doing things is the only problem. It's always worse in the mind than it is in the real world. (Look out there at all those things we dread doing!)

"There, that wasn't so bad, was it?" How many times have our teachers, our parents, our doctors, or our friends said those words to us? Hundreds. Thousands. Did we make a note? Did we let it sink in?

Don't dread anything anymore. Just jump in and do it. If you're stuck with what you're writing, keep your hands moving. You are the author of your life. Keep your hands moving. You are co-writing your co-written love song with the universe today. So keep your hands moving.

Motivation is inner movement. People get confused about motivation and think they need to have it before they can get their lives into motion.

Not so. Motivation most often shows up later, when you're

already halfway into things.

Yet I run into people all the time who are trying to figure out ways to get motivated to do something they have been putting off.

Patricia was just such a person. She was a client of mine who was going to write a major corporate proposal, and she kept putting it off.

"How do I get myself motivated to do it?" she asked.

"You don't have to."

"What? How do you mean?"

"It's one of the great misconceptions of life that motivation has to occur *before* you do a task. I'm going to prove to you that it does not," I said.

"Okay, this I've got to see, because I've been trying to get myself motivated to do this thing for two weeks now."

"Good. So are you ready to experiment?"

"Yes!"

"You have a proposal to write, correct?"

"Correct."

"How long do you think it will take you?"

"Maybe four hours. Maximum. If I do a final edit."

"Okay. Here's what I want you to do. Ready? Will you do it?"

"Of course."

"Hang up the phone and write the proposal, and call me as soon as it's finished."

And then I hung up the phone. Why waste more of her time?

The next morning Patricia called me.

"It's finished. I sent it off by FedEx."

"Wonderful!"

"But I wasn't very happy with you for a while there."

"No doubt."

"Why did you have to do it that way?"

"I wanted the drama. Sometimes I like it when we do things together that you will remember always."

"What was your point in doing that?"

Patricia already knew what my point was, but she wanted to hear it from me. She wanted to talk it through because beneath her irritation she was actually excited. She had found something she didn't know she had.

What was it? Was it her action switch? Was it a little button she could push to get the whole body moving? Well, yes and yes! She found out she had the ability to move into action any time she wanted. Only a thought stood in the way. And when she saw it was only a thought and not *the truth about life*, she could let it just arise and dissolve as all thoughts do when we don't cling to them. She now knew she could do things with or without the "motivation" or even the desire to do them. She found she could just do it. Allow it to be done.

She also found out something equally exciting. About fifteen minutes into writing her proposal she was filled with fresh energy for writing it. It was as if a pump had been primed.

People think the mind must shift *first*, before any bold, creative action can be taken.

It's nice when it does, but it's not necessary.

You can shift the body first instead, and the mind will eventually follow. That's why Natalie Goldberg says that a writer simply needs to move her hands. The mind will catch up.

Emerson put it this way, "Do the thing, and you shall have the power."

People tell me, "I don't know if I have it in me to write a book."

I say, "I know what you mean, I never had it in me, either."

"Then how have you written your books?"

"Some of them longhand on paper, and some on the keyboard of a computer."

"That's not what I'm asking."

"I know, but that's what I did. That's how I did it."

"Where did you find the motivation?"

"Somewhere during or after the keystrokes or the pen strokes. Sometimes after five minutes, sometimes after fifty. I realized it never mattered. It was just a superstition to think that it mattered."

Do everything you want to do in this life. Don't wait till you find the motivation to do it. Stop looking for the "passion" first.

Self-help evangelists are always crowing about finding your passion and living with passion and intention, and I get tired of listening to all that. All that inflated rhetoric is quite unnecessary. Just do the thing you want to do.

The mind shifts while you're doing it.

The philosopher Shima Morita said, "Effort is good fortune." He realized that satisfaction in work came not so much from finding the "perfect" job but rather from "doing the job in front of you perfectly."

Just as appetite comes by eating,
so work brings inspiration, if inspiration
is not discernible at the beginning.

~ **Igor Stravinsky**

16

The rare magic of self-reliance

Sometimes I will ask a person to write down the one area in life they would like to get better at. What is it for you? What is the talent, skill, or ability that you would like to get better at? That one certain skill that—if you mastered it—you know it would bring success your way?

Almost everyone can identify the skill. So they write that down.

Now, the second thing I want you to write down is, **What's your current practice of that skill?**

"Say what?"

"Yes, write down your *current practice* of that skill."

"What do you mean?"

"What do you currently *do?* Regularly?"

And that's where people give me the blank stare.

"I don't practice that."

Okay. Game over.

If I were actually willing to see myself as a creator, I would *create* habits and tendencies through practice. Directed, enthusiastic practice. Of any skill or craft important to my profession.

People say that we were created in the image of our creator. So many different spiritual disciplines will tell you this . . . and "so in just this way you are a child of God."

Well, if that's true, then my business and my life ought to be about creating!

If I'm created in the image of my creator, then I will create. I will not react. I will create. Including creating skillfulness where I want to be skillful.

Let the beauty we love
be what we do.

~ **Rumi**

17

What have we done to money?

Around the pure loving energy that money is, we have wrapped beliefs such as shortage, obligation, hard work, loss, manipulation, security and survival. We have then wrapped layers of emotional consequences such as fear, frustration, anger and shame.

~ Arnold M. Patent

This is an "insecure"-looking universe! How beautiful that it all changes daily. It ebbs and flows and comes and goes. The tide comes in and the tide goes out.

And such good tidings come to all who can see that clearly.

Because then it's possible to welcome the "hard times" because they allow us to rise up and play well. They allow us to renew our comprehension of money as pure, loving energy that flows to those who best serve others.

The award-winning novelist Walker Percy had some very interesting questions about this paradox. He asked:

"Why do people often feel so bad in good environments that they prefer bad environments?"

"Why is a man apt to feel bad in a good environment, say Short Hills, New Jersey, on an ordinary Wednesday afternoon? Why is the same man apt to feel good in a very bad environment, say an old hotel on Key Largo in a hurricane?"

I think we know the answer to these questions.

Challenges and problems can give us a new feeling of life.

Standing beside you, with my arm around you, in that old hotel in Key Largo, with the hurricane winds and rain whipping at the windows, we had adventure. That sense of wild challenge, dancing with the elements; we really felt *alive* again. Our minds were shifting all by themselves.

I can allow that same context of adventure to flow in to my "problems with money." The same way I felt when I was a small child entering a new field of play.

Because we think our happiness comes from getting what we want, we pursue goals at the cost of our relationships, our health, and our spiritual well-being.

~ **Michael Neill**

18

Some goals can turn against you!

If you focus too much on the *outcome* you want to achieve, that goal can turn on you—like a formerly friendly house pet who has become vicious.

Soon the formerly optimistic prospect of hitting that goal turns to fear . . . fear of not achieving it. Soon the very sight of the goal becomes a drag—it reminds you that *thus far* you are a failure, because you're so far away from achieving what you really want.

You walk into your room, look up at the big goal on the whiteboard, and it says to you: NOT THERE YET!

And this is not a good place to come from. Fearing not achieving something you made up to begin with!

Soon this fear shuts down all playful, creative activity in your mind. The best things the mind has to tap into are driven out by worry. Intuition disappears. You contract into a small self, and that self feels like the trembling heart of a captive bird.

It might be time to embrace the concept of *process* versus *outcome*. Process goals are all doable throughout your day. Like sending out three business proposals today, or doing twenty pushups. These are action items. You can *always* achieve them and feel the satisfaction and fulfillment of having done so. (And, paradoxically, they will get you to your outcome faster than focusing the mind on the outcome goal will. Outcome goals can often push your outcome away from you.)

If my outcome goal is to weigh 175 pounds by September 1, then I want to go immediately to *process*. The outcome exists only to shape and inform the process. What might my daily process goals be? To log 10,000 steps a day on my pedometer? To keep my carbohydrate intake at a certain number of grams? To record that daily victory in a food journal? To avoid flour and sugar, just for today? To weigh myself daily? (What gets measured in life gets done.) All of this is *process*.

Anyone can work a process. Anyone can do this for a day, and this day is all I have anyway, it's the only leverage point I can *ever* operate from. If I am going to eventually weigh 175, it will be because of some process I do *today*.

This is good news, because the long-term outcome can flip on me from inspiring to intimidating. One low mood, one micro-shift down the ladder will do it. But a mind that shifts to "just for today" eliminates intimidation and achieves whatever it wants.

Loneliness is the poverty of self;
solitude is the richness of self.

~ May Sarton

19

You've got to go out of your mind

Most people try to improve who they are. They even call it self-improvement. But that's their whole problem. The "self" they think they are improving is only a transparent web of personalized stories.

The story called "you" is nothing but an empty patchwork of grievances from the past and fearful victim thoughts in the present. And it's those victim stories that give birth to new, anxious expectations for the future.

You can't create something beautiful from that position. You can't make a clear, pure-as-water commitment while being dragged down by a sad sack full of personal history. You have to allow a shift out from under that heavy mindset completely. Then you'll see a dropping of all grievances and expectations.

The samurai warriors called it "no mind."

Jason Lezak agrees. He was the oldest man on the U.S. swimming team, and he pulled off one of the great comebacks in Olympic history, hitting the wall just ahead of France's Bernard in the 400 freestyle relay, a race performance so fast it actually erased two world records. Few Olympic events live up to the hype, but this one exceeded it. The thirty-two-year-old Lezak was nearly a body length behind Bernard as they made the final turn, but the American hugged the lane rope and stunningly overtook him on the very last stroke.

"I knew I was going to have to swim out of my mind," Lezak said. "Still right now, I'm in disbelief."

He was out of his (personal) mind.

Or as Jim Manton says in his powerful book, *The Secret of Transitions*:

"To transition we must enter a state in which we are no longer what we once were, and yet we are not who we must become. We have to be willing to stand in the open gap and momentarily risk being nothing."

Every time we choose safety,
we reinforce fear.

~ Cheri Huber

20

Just allow your games to begin

People can improve their careers faster if they relate their careers to a game. Or a playful contest . . . or a Bruce Lee martial arts tournament.

They need to take it out of the category of "grim reality" and put it into the game mentality, so it can free them up to find their best thinking.

So today I'm going to see if I can picture a possible game. Instead of picturing what's wrong with life. That's the whole formula right there.

When I'm depressed, I meditate on one non-transformational mantra: Me. Me. Me. Me. Me. So today I will try a change of course. Rather than obsessing about my unique personality and ego, I will pick a game to play. Once I decide what that is, then I'll just be whoever I want to be to get that game going.

When I hit a speed bump, I might simply step back a little, in prayer or meditation or on a good long walk, and observe the patterns of thought that clouded up my brain and see how all those patterns obscured my spirit. I let them fall away. I love the dissolution. It's beautiful, like fireworks in the sky as they fall and fade.

I want to remind myself that the body takes each thought

and translates it into a feeling, which is a wonderful system if I understand it. If I know how it works, how it always goes thought-to-feeling, then I can allow that awareness to effect a mind shift.

Falling out of self-centered, self-conscious seriousness, I fall in love with the game.

As the traveler who has lost his way, throws his reins on his horse's neck, and trusts to the instinct of the animal to find his road, so must we do with the divine animal who carries us through this world.

~ Ralph Waldo Emerson

21

Time to take an extraordinary trip

I love reading Robert Godwin's *One Cosmos* wherein he says that enlightenment is sometimes as simple as a completely relaxed and open body.

Once my suffocating story of a permanent lazy personality is dropped (not by doing anything, but by *seeing it* as a made-up story), I can experience the fresh courage to see that there's really nothing wrong with me whatsoever. That I've got everything I need for now, and the only question is what *action* is next.

Because in action, higher intuition occurs and great ideas for even greater action occur.

You can just test this out for yourself. Let's say you say that your "personality" is such that you lead a kind of lazy, sedentary lifestyle. "I'm always just answering emails and watching TV—that's just what I'm like. It's who I am and what I'm like."

Now you feel stuck.

But instead of looking at it that way, why not just take action? When you're in action, new intuition flows right into you and you can see new areas to go. Check this out. If you're stuck—you "don't know" what to do next—but all that's needed is to move! To get into motion!

Our bodies were designed to move. They were designed to

dance and walk and play. Just watch kids on a playground if you forget what the body was designed to do—just look out the window and watch them for a while. They won't be sedentary. Their inner intuition tells them to jump and sing!

So, I get up and take a walk. I walk around the block. I walk around the office halls. I go up and down the stairs. Soon I'm amazed how my total perspective of thinking is shifting and opening and shifting and opening while I'm in motion.

Oxygen flowing into the brain. All the limbs moving. The old, stuck personality's no longer there because now I'm like an animal in the best sense of the word. And because I'm like an animal I can access that part of me that in animals is called intuition. Instinct!

22

You know how to do commitment

I love people who say "Done" when you request something.

Look at how time disappears when that happens! When the person is committed, the task is not "*going to* be done" in the future; it's done. Already. Done even before it's done!

The task is no longer in the past or in the future, because with commitment, there is no more time. That's why tenses are meaningless in the face of a commitment.

"Can you coach me by phone Friday at 3:00 pm?" someone asks, and I say, "No. I will have just gotten off my plane to New York."

Look at that weird tense. Will have just gotten. It's striving to express something definite and guaranteed! What you're seeing is my commitment to be in New York. It makes mincemeat of time. And tense.

People say, "I'm in New York that week." That's present tense! Why use present tense when it's the future? Because commitment is there. Commitment makes it *already done* right now even though it is technically going to happen in the future.

I know I am going to be on that plane. I've made that commitment. Therefore, in my mind, I'm already there! My mind can shift time. And time is the stuff life is made of.

That's the beauty of a created commitment. Certainty arrives! And certainty is so different than belief. The etymological root of belief is to "fervently hope" something is true. To try to believe in yourself is to fervently hope you can do what you say you can do.

But a commitment is different. It's the internal voice that says, "I am *certain* I am doing this."

No matter what. No matter how hard.

This is already done.

The higher your self-esteem, the more inclined you are to treat others with respect, since you do not perceive them as threats. The higher your self-esteem, the more joy you experience in the sheer fact of being, of waking up in the morning, of living inside your body.

~ **Nathaniel Branden**

23

What would shift my self-esteem?

Knowing the kinds of communication that raise your self-esteem and the kinds that lower your self-esteem can be a wonderful guideline to how you live your day. Because then you can shift from one to the other!

Any time your spoken messages, texts, emails and voicemails lift another person's spirits, you raise your own self-esteem. Because your sense of separateness from others will drop away. The illusion that you are living in isolation disappears. You begin to realize that we are all one team.

And while you enjoy assisting others, you don't mind going against the flow and being your own person either. You aren't out to "please" anybody, so you are free to create your independence. You become more self-reliant by not always trying to fit in. By being willing to buck the trends, your self-esteem rises.

Here's an obituary I read a little while ago that illustrated this point for me. It was for Sir John Templeton. Look what self-esteem did to fill his sails during his very full life! He trusted himself to always see the gift inside every problem.

From *The Economist* in London: "If on any day over the past few decades, you had chanced to be strolling in the early morning at Lyford Cay in the Bahamas, you might have seen a wiry, determined figure power-walking in the sea. Keen as a whippet, his thin arms pumping, he headed into the prevailing swell. In his 80s, he would do an hour of this. In his 90s, he still managed 25 minutes.

"Sir John Templeton spent his life going against the flow. In September 1939, when the war-spooked world was selling, he borrowed $10,000 to buy 100 shares in everything that was trading for less than a dollar a share on the New York Stock Exchange. All but four eventually turned profits. In early 2000, conversely, he sold all his dot com and Nasdaq tech stocks just before the market crashed. His iron principle of investing was 'to buy when others are despondently selling and to sell when others are greedily buying.' At the point of 'maximum pessimism' he would enter, and clean up."

Self-esteem comes from the optimism I allow to bloom inside of me while not buying into the maximum pessimism of others.

Nor should we forget that courage is contagious, that it overcomes the silence and fear that estrange people from one another.

~ **Paul Logat Roeb**

24

A spotless mind will shift faster

*Don't concern yourself with the faults of others. Use the
scouring powder of wisdom to keep the rooms of your own mind
bright and spotless. By your example, other persons will be
inspired to do their own housekeeping.*

~ Paramahansa Yogananda

Unexpected benefits come when I lose interest in the faults of
others. Soon I'm back into my own energy and creativity,
doing small things mindfully. Surprising opportunities are
offered to me when I forget about judging other people. Even
if just for a moment. Because now, free of their faults, I can put
my heart and soul into serving them and caring about them.

What did criticizing others accomplish? Were they ever
grateful for it? Or do people hate, fear and avoid being
criticized and judged?

One thing I do know about people . . . they absolutely love
being inspired. Why not just have *that* be my simple playbook?

Breakthroughs come as a result of shifting your commitment from the predictable future to a possible future.

~ **Werner Erhard**

25

My terror was you'd set me free

There is a radical, controversial, powerful poet named Frederick Seidel. At the beginning of a recent book I wrote I used his lines:

> Don't cure me. Sickness is my me.
> My terror was you'd set me free.

I think those lines express so beautifully what happens when we go to a coach or a therapist or a mentor. We don't really want to be cured of our sick beliefs because we think that's who we are! We get confused and think our sickness is our identity. If I lose that, maybe I'll be nothing. Don't cure me. Sickness *is* my me.

The second line by the poet says, "My terror was you'd set me free."

I know that terror! I felt it before going to Byron Katie's nine-day school. Many people assume Katie is some kind of diaphanous being, a new age priestess with feel-good, pseudo-spiritual rituals for the gullible. Well, not really!

Her work asks that the worker of the work bring great courage to the party. She calls it "the great undoing." One woman stood up halfway through the school and said, "I feel like I'm going to die" and Katie said, "Let's hope you do."

How cruel a thing to say! Or so it would seem. But Katie merely wanted that woman's false identity to die so that her true, healthy, infinite being would be set free to just LOVE EVERYTHING. Terrifying. Sickness was my me. My terror was she'd set me free.

I like these words from John Lennon, from a desolate song he wrote called "Isolation":

> People say we got it made.
> Don't they know we're so afraid?

People thought John and Yoko had it made. They had fame and fortune. They could do anything they wanted. While you and I? Who screams for *us*? And we do things because we HAVE TO! The Beatles had it made.

So why, then, were they so afraid? Why? Can we even imagine the painful isolation that comes with fame? People loving you for all the wrong reasons? People loving you, not because of their true experience of the real you, but because of the fame you have. The mere name and face recognition. Hey, look! Isn't that one of the Beatles? Or is it one of the Beastie Boys? What does it matter? I've just seen a *face*! Can I have your autograph? I want to be able to show it to people back home. I want them to see that I saw someone whose face is famous. What? You're having dinner with your wife? What are you, some kind of snob, better than someone like me?

No wonder it feels like isolation. No wonder he sang, "Don't they know we're so afraid."

But the antidote to all of this isolation and fear is sweet, and fun to watch being put into play. The fearless life is no more than this fearless moment . . . the one your mind will always shift to when you finally know about it. Soon you'll become inseparable from the gentle awareness that shifts your mind to joy.

You won't be upset even when your brain is grinding out in

the gear of personal thought and worry. You'll see it and smile. It's just a train of thought; it's not who you are. And if you can see the train, you're not the train.

Just as in real life, if you're watching a train pull out of the station, you are not on that train.

It's no longer a mystery to understand that a train of thought is only that. Not who I am. But when I believe my thoughts they become like the *Mystery Train* in the song written by Junior Parker and recorded by Elvis, The Band and the Doors:

> Train, train rolling down the line
> Well it took my baby
> And left poor me behind

Things do not change;
we change.

~ **Henry David Thoreau**

26

Considering becoming a millionaire?

Being a millionaire is the best possible thing you can do for society. If you have more, you have more to give. If you are financially independent, then you will not be a financial burden on others. Contrary to what you have been led to believe, your dream of being a millionaire is extremely virtuous.

~ John R. Colt

Well, that sure goes against everything. Don't we just envy and despise millionaires?

My friend Matt Furey has helped more people become prosperous than any one I know. He lives half the year in China, and has obtained a true perspective on how that country has evolved toward progress.

In a recent email from over there, Matt wrote, "China changed its direction when they stopped redistributing the wealth and did as Deng Xiao Ping advised. What did he advise? Two things: 1. To Grow Rich is Glorious and 2. Yi bu fen ren, qian fu qi lai. Translation for #2: If you want the country to prosper, you must let a few people get rich at a time. You CANNOT make everyone rich or prosperous at the same time."

Many of my clients carry a strange guilt about plotting their own financial success. The moment I ask them to picture a successful, prosperous future for themselves, they get nervous. "What about the people who aren't prosperous? Won't it hurt their feelings if I get rich?"

Matt Furey continued, "The other day my wife, Zhannie, told me something I didn't know about her early days in China—before we married: 'When I worked in the factory in China, before the government opened the door and let people make money,' she said, 'everyone got the same pay no matter what. It was 35 dollars a month. So we took our knitting needles to work. And everyone knitted when they were supposed to be working. Everyone in my family can knit. Blankets, sweaters, clothes, you name it. And we'd go home for lunch and stay late. Or we'd sneak outside and play around. We did as little as possible. Everyone was this way. NO ONE worked hard. Everyone told you NOT to do your best because it didn't matter anyway. You got paid the same no matter what.'"

Matt is an expert martial artist and physical trainer, and he's also an expert on teaching people to use the internet to serve people and become wealthy. He is gifted in teaching the proper mind shifts necessary for pessimists to turn their lives around and create prosperity.

He isn't very happy with the U.S. Government right now. "Right now they're imagining nothing but crisis and catastrophe—and they're creating more of it with each passing day. But I wonder what would happen if they changed what they're imagining, what they're communicating, and gave people optimism and hope instead of fear and despair."

The shift Matt recommends will happen. Not from a major government pronouncement, but inside one person at a time. Starting with you. And then me. And then the next person we share optimism with.

Happiness is who we already are,
once our minds are clear.

~ Byron Katie

27

Survey says: Give us a faster horse!

If I had asked my customers what they wanted,
they would have said a faster horse.

~ Henry Ford

Henry Ford didn't end up listening to his customers. He listened instead to his inner voice. His mind shift was a shift from worried poll-taking to a more intuitive, creative voice.

How do people like Henry Ford create great things? By just listening to others? By taking their orders? Or by going into the slowed-down silence of a goof-off day of solitude . . . a glorious day wherein genius thrives and a new idea bursts from the right side of the brain to the newly-harmonized left?

Most people don't create surprising new things in their day. They are too busy trying to do too many timeworn things at once. Most of the people I know think they are starting their day with "too many things to do!"

I started coaching Renata by asking her how her life was. And she said she had too many things to get done and not enough time.

"That's a formula," I said, "for a very miserable, frustrating day."

She asked why. I said it was because she was always trying

to live in the future. Like a fly bouncing against the window pane trying to get into the house. Did you ever see the horror film *The Fly*? That's how most busy people live. Buzzing and pounding against the glass trying to get into their own future. They think it's a better place.

But right now? Right now is a mess for them. Right now is chaos. Right now is a million things to do as Renata fumbles with her cell phone in her car, not noticing the light has changed. She almost blew her mind out in a car! All from having too much to do. And not enough time to do it.

But true, real-world success (not to mention happiness) comes from *not* having too much to do. It comes from only having one thing to do. Just this one thing, right here, right now.

I just do what's in front of me, whatever appears in the moment. I watch and witness: I remain as awareness; I continue to expand without past or future, going nowhere, behind the limits of speed.

~ **Byron Katie**

28

If only I were that beautiful

Most all people wish they were prettier. They think to themselves, "If I were beautiful I'd be happy. If I were rich I'd be happy. If I were rich AND beautiful, like one of those models on TV I'd be *really* happy. I'd have it all."

Okay, but then why did this beautiful young woman I see pictured in the morning paper commit suicide? Twenty-year-old model Ruslana Korshunova jumped to her death from the ninth-floor balcony of her New York City apartment. She had been on the cover of all the top magazines. She was famous. She was beautiful. What could possibly have been that bad?

Here's what was bad: her thinking.

She was (I think we can know this without knowing her at all) troubled by her thoughts. Unable to let thoughts pass her by like clouds. Unable to *not believe* her thoughts. Unable to experience a shift in her mind.

In the accounts I read of her death, all kinds of people rushed around speculating on the circumstances that led to her suicide. A love affair gone wrong? Some major money setbacks? They tried so hard to explain it circumstantially. But they will never find the real reason. Because they don't have her thoughts to examine. They don't know what she was believing.

That's the one part of the CSI work at the suicide scene that will never show up: what she was *thinking*? Because if we knew the thoughts she was believing, we'd see that she really felt she had no choice but to jump, believing what she was believing in the final moment.

The mind shift one experiences that allows disengagement from believing one's thoughts is so liberating that once you've seen it it's hard to imagine going back into those beliefs. It's hard to imagine believing (for very long) the kind of thought that would compel you to jump. It's hard to imagine. It's hard to fully remember the nasty, adhesive (belief) that kept you stuck on the negative thought.

When you unquestioningly believe something negative, there's no shift available. No access to the gear shift in your mind.

When I was a little boy growing up I was scared of bullies. They never really hurt me, looking back. But they scared me. (Isn't it weird how it's always the *thought* of something—the anticipation of it—that brings the worst fear? Never the thing itself. Once the thing itself arrives it's already over and done and we are just okay.)

But because of my inability to shift away from the thought that bullies were real threats to me, I suffered. It's a real enlightened parent who can teach the availability of a mind shift. Not many can even see it for themselves.

So the child—in this case, me—looked for salvation elsewhere. Sometimes in comic books about Mighty Mouse. My hero. I was soon pretending I was Mighty Mouse. Then I was okay. I'd found a new thought, a happy one. (Mighty Mouse represented possibility.) I wrote about the refuge I took in my dependency on Mighty Mouse in the book *Fearless*, and some people have already responded to that by sending me pictures of Mighty Mouse. I wrote that just seeing his picture still made me remember good feelings, so people have sent me his picture, wanting me to feel those good feelings again. I thank you. Just seeing him flying in to save the day allows my mind to remember the feeling. So thank you.

But today I don't have to seek imaginary refuge in a comic book superhero, or in the Avengers, or in a Tony Robbins pep rally. Or in a Beyoncé concert. (Maya Angelou once said, "Music was my refuge. I could crawl into the space between the notes and curl my back to loneliness." Wow.)

But true refuge is not out there. It's within.

Within? Within my ego?

No, it's deeper than that. Below and beyond that. It is prior to thought. Prior to sound. It's in the deep. It's rolling there always.

And you, of tender years,
Can't know the fears that your elders
   grew by,
And so please help them with your
   youth,
They seek the truth before they can die.

~ Crosby, Stills, Nash & Young

29

Why do children teach us so much?

It's fun to watch children. To talk to them and really see how they love to learn and grow. We can observe so much.

Children spend most of their time in the alpha brainwave state. That's why children learn so effortlessly. Notice how they easily learn a second language. As Peter Ragnar says, "All an infant needs to do is listen and imitate. But adults, with an assortment of concerns and mental stresses, struggle with it as if it were a great task. An infant raised in a relaxed, carefree, mentally enriching environment absorbs like a sponge."

Accessing this alpha state is a true mind shift. It happens when we dream. It happens in meditation. It happens during hypnosis. And it happens during any kind of deep relaxation and falling out of personal thinking.

The anxious, left-brained beta state is another story. It's a version of the worried mind most people bring to their day's work. But sometimes just closing your eyes and taking a deep breath and picturing the ocean within can allow the shift that gives you the peaceful idea you've been waiting for.

When fate throws a knife at you
there are two ways to catch it:
By the handle, or by the blade.

~ Chinese saying

30

Catching life by the handle!

Bad news from corporate. Good news from home. Bad news from the world of baseball. Good news from my best client. Bad news from my daughter's school. Good news from my doctor. Bad news from the evening news.

No wonder I am crazy. Swung back from one polarity to the other!

It's a wonder that *everyone* isn't "bipolar"—swinging from the opposite poles all day of bad news and good news.

And to further complicate my thinking, a lot of what I *thought* was bad news last month actually turned out to be good. Bad news that my grandmother fell and hurt herself became good news that she's in a retirement village she now loves, with better safety and companionship.

Why does it happen so often that bad turns to good?

I wish I could *shift my mind* so that it now suspends all judgment! Maybe that would slow things down so that I can always catch the knife by the handle. When it's the bad news knife being thrown at me, I could then handle it because I'd know that I can convert it to something good, eventually, if I give it half a chance and a little imagination. And if it's the good news knife I can just catch it and be grateful. I would win either way.

Rejoicing in ordinary things is not sentimental or trite. It actually takes guts. Each time we drop our complaints and allow everyday good fortune to inspire us, we enter the warrior's world.

~ Pema Chödrön

31

Optimism is a user-friendly program

Once while I was in the airport waiting to fly away, I noticed people running around, frantically opening laptops and chattering into cell phones and dashing from gate to gate. I began to wonder, what are they chasing?

It had to be stories, right? Chasing the stories about the things they think they need. Chasing relationships, money, new cars, granite countertops and validation of their excellent parenting.

I do this, too? Oh yes. Looking for life in all the wrong places. Not understanding the word "within." Not stopping to allow everyday good fortune to inspire me. Drawing my sword and seeking better kingdoms in distant lands.

And why do I forget that the kingdom is already here? It's the kingdom that has been described for thousands of years as "within."

I'm here in Atlanta working with my clients at a large company to show them that the technology of the mind (that knows how to shift) can match their peerless technology on the factory floor. Or at least that's the language I use to avoid sounding like a practitioner of new-age, "soft" training.

I'm showing them on a slide that the brain can use the "technology of optimism" as a proven biocomputer program to open up creativity and solution-thinking.

And without such a shift? They will buy into the common (erroneous) wisdom that says optimism is a personality trait you're either born with or not. Like a hardwired sunny disposition. And the "optimist" in the common, everyday perception is a happy, glad-handing idiotic, beaming, smiling, false front of upbeat mannerisms.

Actually, optimism is tougher than all that. Optimism, when it's real, is a powerful, precise, teachable tool for unlocking the right side of the brain—and all its practical functions.

Dr. Martin Seligman conducted studies of over half a million people for twenty years. He scientifically validated two important findings in those studies: 1) Optimism is more effective than pessimism, and 2) Optimism can be learned.

Shocking. It can be learned! Aren't we stuck with our personalities? If a person is moody, is she not permanently moody? As permanent as her blue eyes?

Goodness, no. When you read *Learned Optimism* you learn that you can dispute—DISPUTE!—any pessimistic thought that appears. It's nothing permanent. It can disappear like a rain cloud across the sky of your mind.

Dispute it. Challenge it. Question it. Make the case for a greater possibility than a thought can hold. Make the case for more options open to you than gloom.

It's as if you had a higher self that you don't call on much. Except in a huge crisis. But if you called on it more and more, it would become more present. It would reveal itself to be . . . the real you.

Because that pessimistic voice in you is a very small blip on the radar screen of who you really are. Why let it rule? Just allow the shift in your mind up to optimism.

Suppose you had no past.
That would be an interesting place to be in.

~ Werner Erhard

32

You can let old memories expire

I used to think that all you had to work with was your existing memory. Sensible? Your mental life is *made* of memories. Correct? What else would you have to work with?

I was proven wrong. I was proven wrong when I went to acting class. My teacher, Judy Rollings, taught something to actors called "the process" in which you *made up* memories.

Hold it right there. How can you *make up* memories? Isn't that a contradiction?

No, because the brain is a wonderful thing. It has something called imagination. To be more modern, we might call the process mental imaging. Now I call it creating.

A teenage boy fantasizes kissing the homecoming queen even though she doesn't know him from Adam. But the boy kisses her in his fantasy during study hall when his eyes are closed and his math book is open.

Then a funny thing happens when the class bell rings and he sees her in the hall. He blushes. He blushes!

Why would he blush if he never really kissed her? (The answer to that question contains the secret to our creativity.)

So Judy Rollings taught her actors a similar process. If you are going to blush on stage, it helps to create a memory that will trigger the blush. So we actors *created* past experiences for our characters to work with. With our eyes closed we made up images and experiences that, upon recollection, felt real.

If you don't like the life you've lived, imagine a new one.

Shift your mind. Watch what happens to the world around you.

Here's an exercise I learned from Dr. Nathaniel Branden when I was his client for some badly needed, just-in-time psychotherapy.

Draw a line on a piece of paper. On the left end of your line put a letter B for birth. Then at the right end of the line put a big letter D for death. Then find where you are now. Don't over-think, just draw a downward slash line somewhere between B and D and have that be your now.

Look at your line. How much life is there left? Between your slash and D? Does it scare you to look at that? Don't let it scare you. Just let it remind you that if you want to do something wonderful, it's now or never. Rise up above that linear line! Create a new memory and act on it.

Remember that living in a linear way only means that life will always be just one damn thing after another. Soon the worm (the personalized ego) gets sick and old crawling on his belly. He is now worming his way across the horizon into old age with a host of newfound fears and worries. Grumpy old man is the best front he can think to put up.

But this is the story of you! This is your life when you buy into the flatliner's story. Permanent, unchangeable memories, right? You're born. Things happen. And you die. Tragically. In an untimely way. Because linear life always leads to untimely death.

Unless you know you can always *rise up*. Relax the grip you have on your memories. The mind then shifts by itself from horizontal to vertical and you rise up. You can feel this right now.

We waste time
looking for the perfect lover,
instead of creating the perfect love.

~ Tom Robbins

33

Looking for the perfect lover

It's just like the time I was getting ready to go to a football game and looking all over—and I do mean ALL OVER—the house for my binoculars while they were, all the while, around my neck.

We search far and wide for the friends and lovers who will reassure us that we are worth something. Instead of finding the love inside we have to give. Always already there.

But then we make up a story that we need to find it in other people!

But the wonderful psychologist George Pransky teaches about how the mind can shift on this subject of love. And when it shifts, it has a calming effect.

Pransky says, "When anyone has even the slightest inkling of an understanding of the role of thought in creating perception, it has a calming effect. One avoids becoming consumed in a spiraling intensity of their own perceptions. One doesn't get carried away and upset. One goes the other direction, tending to calm down, to get a little humble about it, thinking: Maybe I need to take a fresh look at this, let my intelligence behind my thought evolve my perception, see it in a more understanding, functional light. That is the nature of life: to create more options, more possibilities."

I have a simple life. I mean, you just give me a drum roll, they announce my name, and I come out and sing. In my job I have a contract that says I'm a singer. So I sing.

~ **Tony Bennett**

34

The courage to not be busy

"I know how busy you are," someone said to me the other day. I said I wasn't. I told him that if I was, I would be making a mistake. A "too-busy" person is a lazy, disorganized person.

When I'm too busy I want to realize that I'm just a gal who can't say no.

My friend Jorge was confused. Wasn't the object in life to be busy? Busy with work, busy with family, busy with being busy. Jorge was even trying to associate being busy with success.

People bow down to "busy."

They say, "Wow, I heard about that new account you guys got, so I know you must be VERY busy, so I'll keep it brief." Or they say, "I heard you got married! So you must be too busy to see me like the old days, so maybe we can talk on the phone."

"Busy" is just assumed to be good. But it is not. It isn't the good life.

When I'm "busy" (as I sometimes am . . . by mistakes I make) it means I have been afraid to say "no." I've been trying to please everybody. I am making myself a doormat to people out of fear of not being liked. From that busy-ness I can't truly serve. I can't serve the God within or even ordinary people from there.

Courage is the life force. A natural but thought-obscured state. When it is not obscured, it pushes the flower up through the concrete. The flower was made—just like we were made—to flourish. The courage to push up and break through is always already resting there. Including the courage to say NO to someone who is about to complicate my life.

When I wrote a book on fear it wasn't a book about how to *add* newfound courage to your life. It wasn't about "building up" your courage. You were born with all the courage you'll ever need. The trick is to allow a shift in the mind that just drops those fears you've added on top of the original courage.

It might have started with worries (they're not full blown fears yet, but they're getting there). First you notice you can drop the worries. Now there's no place for these ridiculous fears to start from.

Maybe you were scared when you watched *The Wizard of Oz*, but soon you realized that monkeys can't really fly. Deep down in your natural courage you now allow yourself to know that.

Fears are paper tigers. You can do anything you decide to do. You can act to change and control your life; and the procedure, the process is its own reward.

~ Amelia Earhart

35

The dazzling mind shifts into systems

I was in Chicago not long ago to work with an elite leadership team at Microchip Technology, a global leader in the field of microcontroller and analog semiconductors. Very exciting.

What sets that company apart is its deliberately created culture. At the heart of that culture is a commitment to work with systems—and to see the underlying system beneath everything.

They emphasize the use of the word "perfect" when describing a system. Every system is perfect for what it produces. Once your mind shifts up to see the perfection in every system, you are in a creative enough state to produce new systems that get different results.

Even if there's a situation (rare at that company) when customers are upset. They say, "We have a perfect system right here for angering the customer." They apply this systems thinking to anything they don't like and want to immediately fix: "We have a *perfect system* for producing poor-quality products, excessively long R&D Development cycles, low margins, unreliable computer networks, low productivity, high turnover," and so forth. (It's all explained in the book written about this company, *Driving Excellence* by Michael Jones and

Steve Sanghi.)

By declaring the existence of a system, they avoid the normal human habit of blaming other *people* for things going wrong. Nothing can ever be fixed or strengthened that way.

Their point is that you'll always get what you've designed a system to get. Therefore the solution to any chronic problem is to design a new system. As opposed to blaming people and making people wrong. This is called "systems thinking" and it's a higher order of thinking than we normally do. It asks for a true mind shift. But once the mind has shifted to systems, the world changes for the better.

We are usually trapped by fear in a very low-level form of judgmental thinking. We blame others. The systems shift solves that.

Almost all the companies I have worked with have ongoing problems with the politics, ego and arrogance (Insecurity) of certain managers. These companies feel that you're always going to have that. The price and pain of working with people!

Not so, says Microchip. At Microchip they see it differently. At Microchip, politics, ego and arrogance are—are you ready for this?—"not allowed." They're not allowed. In other words, NOT ALLOWED!!!

That's pretty simple. And bold. Can you really do that? Well, yes: it's called a deliberately created culture. The old mindset that everyone accepts is that politics, ego and arrogance will simply be a fact of life. People tell you in weary voices: "Get used to it."

But at Microchip those things are simply not allowed—in the same way that wearing a bikini to work is not allowed. When it's really clear that something is not allowed, people just don't do it.

What are you and I allowing? What are we tolerating? What system would we like to create that would produce a different result? That's a mind shift out of victimization into infinite creativity.

Power doesn't come from knowledge. What people know doesn't make them powerful. It's being present to what you're dealing with that gives you power.

~ **Werner Erhard**

36

If you're not enough please stand up

When you take the merely linear road, nothing will ever be enough. When you strive and struggle to live out a story's narrow path from birth to death, nothing you do will ever feel like it's enough.

"I love the way you've fixed up your house! It's so charming!"

But you say, "We're not done yet. We've just got started. There's so much to do. It's really a mess."

"Oh." And here I thought it looked great.

It's a story that some people can't shake loose no matter what. It's the story of not enough.

If I tell you, "You've done well at your job," you don't agree. You say, "I really want a Division Manager position. I should have had it a year ago."

Okay. You look good, though. You've lost weight. I tell you, "You look like you've lost a lot of weight."

You say, "Not enough. Not nearly enough!"

I remark later how well your son is doing in school. I heard he almost made the honor roll.

"Well . . . yes. But he's having some problems in math that we can't seem to solve."

So he's not enough. Even your beautiful son is not enough.

Sometimes just standing up will take you out of your

horizontal "not enough" story and into the real vertical universe of *always enough for now*. It's a true mind shift. The mere act of standing on your feet forces oxygen into your lungs that wasn't there before.

Elizabeth Barrett Browning said, "He who breathes more air lives more life."

Ask your class to stand and take a breath. Look how the stagnant story they were stuck in disappears and they look so fresh and relieved. Relieved! Relieved of bored thought. Relieved of a mind mired in the tales from the crypt of not enough.

Those who do not move
do not notice their chains.

~ **Rosa Luxemburg**

37

The coyote never has a bad day

The past few years have been exciting to walk myself and many of my clients out of the dark regions of fear (imagining a scary future) and into the light (present-moment opportunity).

Most people take their most unpleasant memories of the past and try to let their worried mind paint a future scenario out of that. But your past history does not have to be you. You are free.

I was talking with my friend, the award-winning songwriter and comedian Fred Knipe, about how beautifully *disputation* dismantles negative beliefs we hold about ourselves and others and about life and death. He agreed with me that once we stop believing those frightening thoughts, the mind clears up and there is no more stress. The story about anxious, frightful life is gone. And we are free to act and create anything we want. Or just relax into quiet, happy feelings.

(Most of my life I had done the opposite. I scared myself with stressful beliefs about time, death and money. And how people don't "get" the seriousness of my situations. None of that was ever true. Yet believing it was true made me a stressful believer. I had designed a perfect system for a stressful life.)

In talking to Fred about all this I whimsically sent him these words for my tombstone:

Here lies a stressful believer
who created hell on earth
for himself
and others
out of his
unquestioned thought system

Fred wrote back "That could be on everyone's tombstone. They could just start making generic tombstones with those words on it."

And then Fred said something profound and strange (and very beautiful):

> The coyote has no tombstone. Because the coyote never has a bad day. Neither does the coyote have a good day. Hungry all day is not a bad day. Napping all day full of rabbit is not a good day. Because the coyote has no judgment. He does not evaluate. No 'good for me, bad for me.' He avoids harm and seeks benefit without evaluation, so for him there is neither time nor eternity. People are the only ones who evaluate, and they never stop. It may seem a curse, this process of deciding everything, of pushing all experience through a buzz saw which divides into good and bad, but the curse finally lifts when the evaluation machinery is turned back on itself. When the *experience* of evaluation becomes the subject of evaluation, it becomes clear that without judgment we would become like the coyote.

What does Fred know about the coyote? Maybe more than most people! He is a four-time Emmy-award winning writer for PBS's show, *The Desert Speaks*. So he has written about all the desert flora and fauna. But maybe never quite this deeply. And it was off the top of his head.

Fred also writes songs and performs comedy for a living, and if you ever need a good laugh to pick you up, go to his website and click on one of the many hilarious little routines he does there as his comic alter-ego, Dr. Ludiker. Go here:

www.fredknipe.com

Don't be lured into thinking your own comic alter-ego is false. It is always much closer to the real you. The you that laughs and makes others laugh is more real and true to life than the stressful believer.

Two men look out the same prison bars;
one sees mud and the other stars.

~ Beck

38

You can become a liberated circle

The great novelist Vladimir Nabokov was the first person I know of to point out that a spiral is a liberated circle.

A mind full of expectations is nothing but a vicious circle. Stories about how others don't appreciate me add weight to this vicious circle.

Soon this mind of mine is grinding like a sports car stuck in first gear, crying out to be shifted.

My own mind cries out to be shifted when I'm in some vicious circle story about how *you should be* acting. When SHIFT HAPPENS the circle is liberated. It is now a spiral . . . opening languorously upward in a heavenly swirl, and there is no upper limit.

In the courses I teach on mind shifting I use Nabokov's observation that a spiral is a liberated circle. I draw the vicious circle of an unshifted mind on the white board. Then I draw a spiral. Up from fear and anger and worry and resentment. Up toward creativity, compassion and spirit. There's a gold mine in that sky. And up there at the top, beyond the gold mine, there is even more . . . things too wonderful to even talk about in linear language, or sentences that have beginnings and endings.

What keeps us trapped so low and so far away from that level?

Thinking there are "other" people. Thinking negative thoughts about those people. Unwillingness to forgive other people for being human.

There is an old saying that pretty much says it all: "To forgive is to set a prisoner free and discover the prisoner was you."

When I lived in solitude in the country I noticed how the monotony of quiet life stimulates the creative mind.

~ **Albert Einstein**

39

It is the sheer amount of time put in

Malcom Gladwell's great and intriguing book, *Outliers*, talks about how many hours the Beatles played together before they became famous. Much more than other bands of their time.

They started out obscurely in the city of Hamburg, Germany.

Gladwell says:

> And what was so special about Hamburg? It wasn't that it paid well. (It didn't.) Or that the acoustics were fantastic. (They weren't.) Or that the audiences were savvy and appreciative. (They were anything but.) **It was the sheer amount of time the band was forced to play.**

Here is John Lennon, in an interview after the Beatles disbanded, talking about the band's performances at a Hamburg strip club called the Indra:

> We got better and got more confidence. We couldn't help it with all the experience playing all night long. It was handy them being foreign. We had to try even harder, put our heart and soul into it, to get ourselves over. In Liverpool, we'd only ever done one-hour sessions, and we just used to do our best numbers, the same ones, at every one. In Hamburg we

had to play for eight hours, so we really had to find a new way of playing.

Gladwell reports that the Beatles ended up traveling to Hamburg five times between 1960 and the end of 1962. By the time they had their first burst of success in 1964, they had performed live an estimated 1,200 times, which is extraordinary. Most bands today don't perform 1,200 times in their entire careers.

In my book *Reinventing Yourself* I asked readers to consider taking possession of the most powerful secret weapon in the world. That secret weapon is called practice.

And it is, indeed, a secret to (I'm guessing this number based on my observations) 93.1 percent of America. Pick it up and you'll give yourself what feels like an unfair advantage over everyone else you know.

Malcom Gladwell's book cites case after case where people who we thought simply had amazing talent actually, like the Beatles, had *practiced* more than anyone else. What a strange secret to uncover.

It may turn out that one of my favorite sayings is more true than we realized: Only the disciplined are free. It's only when I am *un*disciplined that all my time gets taken up with distraction. And there's no freedom or mastery in that. Freedom and mastery arise from practicing my profession's most useful discipline.

The drops of rain
make a hole in the stone
not by violence but by oft falling.

~ Lucretius

40

Let this ladder shift your mind

When two people get together in a coaching session, you now have the brain power, the mind power, the soul power, the life power of *two* human beings working together. It's not so much one plus one as it is two squared.

You may say, "Why would one need a coach for that? Why doesn't that synergistic power just happen every time *any* two people talk together or get together?"

Because they're not consciously there to produce change.

In fact, quite often they're there to belabor a conflict! That's why so many relationships slowly go south. They lapse into conflict. One person wants and expects so much from the other person that disappointment becomes the theme.

But in coaching, mind shifting occurs upward. Because the minds are after the same thing.

Some people also have a shift occur in a musical setting when they are in tune with the vibrations of the song. Other people when they exercise. Toby Estler wrote a book on the spiritual power of getting out there and running. When the body is open, the spirit enters.

Sometimes I draw a ladder to illustrate this phenomenon. People who see the ladder suddenly have a visual picture of what's happening inside their mind. Previously they wondered "Why am I stuck?" Or: "Why is life not seeming to work for me?"

Now they can see that the answer is pretty simple and open. They are low on their ladder!

But this ladder—a ladder of human consciousness—can be ascended, with a series of shifts in the mind.

This is hard to see when you are stuck in your own story and stuck in your own belief system.

So I draw the ladder, either on a piece of paper or on the whiteboard, and at the very bottom of the ladder I put the word "death." (I want people to be mildly shocked into a realization that that would be their lowest level of consciousness. I then say after writing the word DEATH at the bottom of the ladder, "If you are trying to persuade someone at *this* level of consciousness to purchase something from you, you've got to be surreally good.")

The next step up is fear. Fear is the next step up from death. It's almost the lowest possible level of living human consciousness. It is really where everything stops. If we could see that and understand it, we would understand people so much better!

We'd understand ourselves so much better, too. We'd shift. Because once that first shift happens, up from fear, all the other shifts are now possible. Courage returns. (We were born with it.) And courage is the virtue that makes all the other virtues possible.

We are done with hope and honor,
We are lost to love and truth,
We are dropping down the ladder
rung by rung.

~ **Rudyard Kipling**

41

All my anger comes from fear

Anger is a mask for fear. It's a way people transmute fear. So whenever you're angry, know that it's based on a fear. It was caused by a fear. There's no way that you could be angry without feeling threatened. The two can't exist apart from each other.

Anger feels more powerful than fear. That's why people execute the mind shift. It's a way that the ego strengthens itself so that it feels like it finally has a little power around this fear.

Because I feel helpless when I just feel the fear. Helpless is not a great feeling. It doesn't hold a candle to being royally ticked off.

So now I am angry and I can push my focus outside of me to an object. I can now identify who or what I want to blame. There's got to be somebody causing this fear in me! It's *you*, or it's the corporation, or it's the government, or it's the market, or it's some other person.

Now go up the ladder a step higher and you'll find resentment. A less dangerous form of anger. It's milder but more ongoing. It can permeate the day. If I resent this person, it can pull me down, creatively and energetically, every time I think of him. It disconnects me from any possibility of enthusiasm.

Enthusiasm? It's the place where all great things in life are created. Emerson saw this. "Nothing great," he said, "was ever created without enthusiasm."

When you jump to the highest part of the ladder, way, way up there, way above worry, resentment, anger, fear and death, there is spirit. There is absolute enthusiasm, there is humor, creativity, joy, and infinite energy, and that's where we want to keep allowing the shifting to take us, because when we can access that (the ultimate mind shift) problems look hilarious. Problems really look like the funniest things we could think of. They're not "real" problems anymore. They're just an adventure.

And that comes from the ultimate mind shift to the very highest level.

This ladder is something I draw so people can actually get a picture of *where they are,* vertically, at any given moment. Where am I? Am I down low? Stuck in worry or fear? If so, I'm not accessing my creativity, or my greatest energy, or my imagination (those states of mind are high on top of the ladder).

Creativity doesn't live down on the lower rungs. Those are the rungs that keep me stuck. I only see yes and no, black and white, bad and good—a narrowly critical mindset trapped in a small part of the linear left side of the brain.

But if I can shift and go! Oh man! I'll be in spirit, I'll be in creativity, I'll be in joy. Now I'll keep shifting so my life opens up. So I can expand myself into that joy I felt when I was young, because that was the real me. I knew it at the time.

I don't actually have to shift before I take good action. I can take the good action in a low mood. I don't have to wait. And sometimes just getting into the game allows thought to drop away, and the rising up the ladder happens on its own.

People say that what we're all seeking is a meaning for life. I don't think that's what we're really seeking. I think that what we're seeking is an experience of being alive.

~ **Joseph Campbell**

42

What are we really seeking?

I like that quote by Joseph Campbell, who wrote *The Power of Myth*.

An experience of being alive. How would that feel?

Joseph Campbell was a very powerful seeker. He went away for five years and just checked out of normal societal life. He took a stack of books with him and dug deeper and deeper into the question of life's meaning. Ultimately he found something really powerful to share with the world.

When he emerged, it seemed like he had the world's entire mythology in his mind and at his fingertips. He then wrote and delivered wonderful principles from the power of mythology to help call people to action, to wake them up to their own possibility of heroic missions. His stories inspired people to do all kinds of things that they would never have done without his inspiration.

One of the greatest things about true mind shifts like Joseph Campbell's is that they are so often followed by real experience. If I read a book that shifts my mind I'm now more eager to try a new experience. As I'm reading I'm whispering "Wow," and I'm highlighting, underlining and taking notes. I might even be calling out to my partner, "Listen to THIS!"

The same thing can happen watching a movie. There are some movies that are so very inspiring that way, that I notice that when I come out of the movie theater, my understanding of the world has shifted. Movies like *Man on Wire* do that for me.

I remember once I went to hear Spalding Gray speak. You might remember him—he did a few movies of his monologues. One was called *Swimming to Cambodia* and it was a movie of just him sitting at a desk talking (which is amazing that it held your interest for so long). Gray would take these talks on the road and he would be up on stage sitting at a desk, and he would just talk to the audience. He was storytelling—about his life, about things that were important to him, about his experience as an actor being in these movies. And it was absolutely spellbinding.

I first saw him do this many years ago before I ever wrote a book or ever gave a talk. I was sitting in the audience at the University of Arizona. I had a job at the time—I can't remember if it was sports writing, or advertising or something like that—where I was getting by utilizing a very small percent of my potential—a small per cent of my creativity, and thinking I was doing the safe thing. (I did not know back then how ultimately suffocating safety can be.)

However, when I sat there in the audience, while Spalding Gray gave his talk (with the audience *loving* it) everything inside my mind shifted! What a strange feeling that was. I stared at him up there on the stage and I thought. "That's me! He is who I am. He's calling me to *be him* by example."

That's one of the things that heroes can do for us. Joseph Campbell got that so right. They can call us to the higher self. And there's always a higher self no matter where you are on the ladder. Your evolution is always a shift. It's not always exactly like a sports car where there's only so many gears. The beautiful thing about the mind is that there's never an end to it. There's always another shift the mind can make.

When I walked out of the theater that day my life was forever changed.

When I came out of the theater, I was with friends and they were saying, "Wasn't that wonderful—didn't you enjoy that?" but I was in another world. It was as if I couldn't even speak. "What's wrong with you, Steve, what's the matter?"

"I just . . . I've just been overwhelmed."

"Well he wasn't *that* good."

"No, no, it's not that—it isn't him, it's me. I'm doing the wrong thing. I'm not doing what I could be doing."

"What are you talking about?"

"He was it. That's me. I want to be sharing things like that, helping people and entertaining them along the way. Or entertaining people and helping them along the way. I don't even know what I want, but it's not what I'm doing."

They said "All right . . . wow, heavy . . . whatever," and I couldn't explain what I meant without looking neurotic. Perhaps I was!

But it wasn't long before I was doing my version of Spalding Gray. May he rest in peace and know somewhere that I am forever grateful.

There was a definite process by which one made people into friends, and it involved talking to them and listening to them for hours at a time.

~ Rebecca West

43

Follow the bliss,
not the expectations

Expectations are stories we believe about how others should behave. Yet, the more expectations I have the more I set myself up for disappointment.

Because with no expectations, there can be no disappointment, only enjoying life as it is and the people in it.

But listen to this: "I expect you to clean your room!"

Imagine yourself hearing those words. A knot forms in your stomach. Your throat tightens a little. Your chest feels like someone is pushing on it. You begin to mentally explore the consequences of rebellion. Because people rebel against expectation.

That's why *creating agreements* is so much more effective. No expectations, just agreements. Two people co-author the agreement in the same way that John Lennon and Paul McCartney would co-author a song. We sing with their song, "And, in the end, the love you take is equal to the love you make."

Parents live in a constant state of anger and anxiety when they expect so much from their children. I know a woman I will call Courtney who walks around all day riddled with expectations for her children. She also has expectations for her husband. So she is in a constant state. And if she died tomorrow her tombstone would say, "DISAPPOINTED."

Take now, however, the example of a different wife and mother I know named Alexandra. Alexandra has no expectations. All human behavior is an amusing surprise to her. And her son's room is clean. How is that happening?

Because she has an agreement with her son about the room.

People are controlled by expectations . . . their own and those of others. It keeps them from ever growing into who they could be. Happy, creative and free.

Most people (and when I say most people, I'm not saying I'm different, I'm talking about myself for most of my life! So, when I say "most people," don't think I am looking down at others—they're me!) . . . so, most people live desperate lives based on expectation.

They wake up in the morning and they put their sensors out and ask themselves subconsciously, "What do people expect of *me* today?" and then they try to live up to all that. It becomes a life run totally by other people's expectations. Or the imagined expectations of others.

What does my boss expect? What does my partner expect? What do my kids expect?

I was talking to someone the other day who was thinking of joining a singing group. For him it would be a revitalizing, self-nurturing experience. Only two days a month would he do this, but he finally said, "I ultimately can't do it because one of my children is involved in softball and I would not want to miss even one day of that because she expects it."

Does he know that for sure? Would that little girl later in life say that she would have wanted her father to give up his singing to not displease her for one moment?

If I spend all my time trying to live up to others' expectations, it's a no-win situation. Because I can never fully do it. They'll just keep adding more expectations. Not only that—if I'm living my life based on living up to other people's expectations, I will sink down my ladder and live all day in the low, slow gear of resentment.

I will always resent, subconsciously, the people whose expectations I am trying to live up to. I mean really, who are *they*? Deep down I know this spirit of mine that says, "Who *are* they? Who are *they* to have me try to live up to their expectations all day? Do I never get my independence? Do I never get to be my own person?"

I had an agent contact me not long ago to ask if I would write a book called *100 Ways to Win People Over*. I said I would not. Even though they would pay me an advance?

Even though.

I said I wouldn't write that book because I don't think winning people over is a very productive mission. It almost always ends up as a desperately misdirected kind of pursuit. Trying to manipulate the imagined expectations of others and win them over.

If I spent my life trying to impress other people and win them over, when would there be time to serve anyone? Would they pay me for winning them over? Or for serving them well? Which of those two activities do people value the most?

Winning people over in my family is also a non-productive pursuit. Why am I trying to anticipate the mercurial mood shifts of other human beings? Why do I always try to "heal" their most irrational moments?

My mind caves in when I do this. Soon I'm thinking: "Oh, no, he's in a bad mood, what did I *do*? I better do something to put him in a good mood!!! What does he *expect*?"

That's such a frustrating life. Instead, I want to serve! I want to just love and enjoy people.

This is also true at work. I want to create agreements. What should we agree to do here? Instead of "Oh, no, I wonder what he *expects*—is he expecting me to get that report in by Friday? I can't believe that, as overworked as I am."

Joseph Campbell's quest for a joyful life was successful. He found it by studying myth and allowing the heroic in myth to call to him so he could be heroic in his own life. His famous prescription was "Follow your bliss."

People have misapplied that advice. They have used "Follow your bliss" to be a kind of modern narcissistic rallying call to indulge yourself, make yourself feel good for now, let everyone else go hang.

That's not really what it means. When you truly and deeply follow your bliss, you will be in the highest service to others. The two go together.

Commitment is an act, not a word.

~ Jean-Paul Sartre

44

Shift from interested to committed

This mind shift is so powerful it can make your hair stand up: it's the shift from being "interested in" something to being *committed* to it. From dabbling to mastery!

For example, I might be "interested in" losing weight. I might be "interested in" making more money. I might be interested in having a better relationship with my partner and I might be interested in learning how to play the piano. I might be interested in a lot of things, but that level of intention rarely achieves anything.

Or haven't I noticed?

So let's create a reliable mind shift that will solve that for you and me forevermore.

Pretend there is a big whiteboard here and I am drawing a big circle and this big circle is your brain. Now inside the circle I am drawing another smaller circle and that's your *committed place.*

Did you know you had this place in you? You do. Everybody does.

Inside this committed place you have already put certain things. Maybe you don't realize it because you put them there without noticing what you're doing. But if you could shift that unconscious activity to a *conscious* approach it would get exciting. For you. Because once you can reliably and consciously put things in your committed place *you can succeed at virtually any project you are engaged in.*

Let's say you are taking a flight to Chicago. When I talk to you about your upcoming flight to Chicago, I notice something very interesting in your speech pattern. I notice the language of commitment. Your language is definitely coming from that *committed place* in your brain.

You now say to me, "I can't be with you on Saturday, I'm in Chicago that day." That's totally committed language. "I'm in Chicago" is a declaration of fact beyond linear time and any notion of "trying to."

If I ask you, "How do you *know* you'll be in Chicago?"

You say, "I've got my ticket."

"Well, how do you know you'll be at the airport in time?"

"Oh, I'll be on that plane."

There's certainty in that language, because you've put it in your committed place.

But now I find that you are unable to talk to me about anything else that way. Just your plane trip. But when we talk about other things in your life, it's easy to see that none of them are coming from that committed place.

I ask, "Will you be at the meeting Friday?"

You say, "I'll try to be there. Yeah, I think I'm going to be there."

And so you come to the meeting but you are late. You miss a lot of the important set-up conversations in the meeting.

I say, "I'm sorry you were late. You missed some key discussions. What happened?"

"Well, you know, I tried to get here on time, but then the phone lit up just as I was leaving my office, and it turned out to be a really important client, and one thing led to another . . ."

And I can see by that use of language that there was never any commitment.

Because there's such a huge difference between commitment and "just trying." Think back to the difference between life and death.

So anything I've got in my mind that I'm going to *try to do*, I want to acknowledge that there's no commitment in that yet. It's okay. I don't want to have nothing but commitments—I'd go crazy. But I do want to notice there are many things I'm really not committed to at all. Those are always the things that don't get done, or don't get done well.

I do want to know, however, that if I would shift in my mind from "interested in" or "trying to" and go up to a higher level of behavior and a higher level of performance, then I would access commitment. And things would happen. Like never before. And it would be good.

The successful warrior is the average person with laser-like focus.

~ Bruce Lee

45

Are you blind to your true power?

Thinking back on the last ten times you traveled out of town, how often did you miss your flight? How many times did you simply not get to the airport on time to be on the flight you had a ticket for?

For most people the answer would be, "Never. Not once did I miss my flight."

I am the same. I don't miss flights either. Even back in my dysfunctional days before I was aware of mind shifting, I didn't miss flights. Although I couldn't make it to meetings on time, or finish certain jobs on time, I never seemed to miss a flight.

Why is that?

It's because I always put the flight into a different part of my brain. I put it in that little circle we have talked about called the committed place.

It might not be holding very many commitments in there right now. There might just be a few in my life. But that circle can expand. It can be used any time I want. In fact, it could be the best kept secret in the entire brain.

To really understand this circle, let me ask you a question. Tomorrow, when you come to work, will you have a shirt on?

"Well, of course."

"But wait a minute, how do you *know* you will have a shirt

on? What if you are running late and you really want to be to work on time and you've got your pants on and you've got your socks and your shoes on, but you just don't have time to put your shirt on?"

"Well, I'd just . . . well . . . I'd just put it on. I'll always have a shirt on."

"Well, gee, you sound awfully sure of that!"

But can you see *why* you are so sure of that?

It's called commitment. Coming to any social engagement with a shirt on is a commitment. It's not something you are ever "interested in" doing. And it's not something you are just going to "try to do."

People who have children always seem to know for sure that their children are not going to go hungry.

If you ask them, "How do you know that? What if you lose your job? If you lose your job, you wouldn't have any money, and you couldn't buy any food for your kids. They would go hungry, wouldn't they? No job is 100 percent secure."

"Well, I'd do something. I'd find another job quickly."

"What if you couldn't find one?"

"I would find one."

"Well, what if you couldn't?"

"Then I'd find another way to access some money for my kids, or I'd find a way that they would be cared for."

"What if there wasn't another way?"

"There would be. I'd make a way."

Can you hear the commitment in that voice? *There would be.* I'd *make* a way. Nothing would get in the way of that person taking care of their kids. So we have found out that "taking care of my kids" was placed in that circle in the brain called commitment.

Again, let's repeat and recognize the available mind shift: You can put *anything you want* into that place.

It's a total transformation that takes place when a person sees this really clearly. Most people only put a few basic survival or social dignity commitments into that sacred place. But you can put anything there. And when you do, things happen for you that never would have happened.

Commitment is that place you access when the building is burning down and you *are going to find a way out.* You are not thinking, "I'll look for a way out because I'm interested in getting out. I'll try a few things, but if it doesn't work I'll just sit down and burn to death." That's not what happens! You are committed to getting out of this building. Or die trying. Literally. And your thoughts reflect it: "I am definitely out of here!"

Maybe you think you would like to lose a little bit of weight. You tell me, "I'm interested in losing weight, I've always been trying to lose a little weight, I've always worried about my weight."

I hear no commitment at all in that.

So I say, "Let me ask you something. What if Jeff Bezos came in here right now with cameras and said 'I'm going to give you ten million dollars tax free if you lose twenty pounds in four months.' Ten million dollars! Are you willing to take up that challenge?"

I bet you would say yes, of course.

But wait a minute. I thought you said that you had a hard time losing weight.

"No, I'll take the challenge, it will be worth it to me."

"Do you think you will lose the weight? Do you think you'll get the ten million? What are the odds?"

"Well, it's done. Yes, I'll lose the weight. Ten million dollars? Yes. No chance I wouldn't do it."

"How do you *know*, because you've tried to lose weight for years!"

"Well, I just know."

"You just told me that you had such a hard time losing weight and that you've tried for years. You told me you couldn't do it. So how can you *now* say that you *would* do it

with so much certainty in your voice? What happened?"
   Committed place. (For the first time it went into that circle.)

Play the game for more than you can
afford to lose . . . only then will
you learn the game.

~ Winston Churchill

46

How I myself lost twenty pounds

Quite often the human ego gets in the way of what we want to achieve. All these egocentric pursuits of impressing other people, winning people over, feeling important, feeling appreciated—all these ego quests end up with you falling to the bottom of your ladder.

But when you shift your mind and float up and see the big picture from the top of the ladder, you can now look down and see the ego. See it? There it is down there struggling to impress people, struggling to win people over, struggling to live up to other people's expectations. That's the little you.

Sometimes you can seduce your own little ego into helping you find your committed place. Let me give you an example. When John Kennedy was a boy he was in an elite private school in the Boston area and they wore uniforms to his school. The uniforms were very important to those kids, and they got in real trouble if anything happened to the uniform or if they lost part of it—especially the cap.

They had a little cap they all wore. When the boys in the school would walk home together from the school, there was a wall that was almost impossible to climb that the boys challenged each other to climb over. "I'll bet you can't climb over that. I'll bet you can't!" and John Kennedy took his uniform cap and threw it over the wall! He knew he couldn't go home without that cap, so by throwing his cap over the wall, he knew he would climb up over the wall.

Can you see what he did? He threw his cap over the wall. He took something inside himself that he was already committed to (getting home with his whole uniform on so he wouldn't get in trouble)—he took that commitment and he transferred it to climbing the wall. By throwing his cap over the wall, he knew he would climb the wall now.

That was a beautiful example of how intuitive kids can be to continuously access higher levels of mind power. Obviously he wasn't thinking at that age in terms of commitment.

But he threw the cap over the wall.

I've always loved that story and I've always thought of ways in my life where I could throw my own cap over the wall so that I'd be automatically coming from my committed place.

So last year in my mastermind meeting (we have twenty people who sit together) I thought of a way to do it. I had noticed walking into one of the earlier meetings that I felt overweight, at least in my own mind, compared to where I wanted to be.

I announced to the group that three meetings from now—in other words, ninety days from now—if I have not lost twenty pounds, everybody in the room will receive $1,000 in cash. It will be on the table in front of you.

Prior to announcing this I had written my exact current weight on the white board. I put the number up there for everyone to stare at. I pointed at it. I said "If three meetings from now the number I write is not twenty less than this number you'll find $1,000 at your table."

Now I knew I would lose the weight. I had thrown my hat over the wall.

I know that this was radical. There are gentler and more self-compassionate ways to get things done than what I did. But I use the story to remind myself that deep down there's always something I can call on.

47

I heard the news today oh boy

I wake up in the morning, the clock radio comes on, and here's the latest bad news—it's the first thing I hear!—my poor mind, my poor brain has to make sense of it and integrate it. It's hard.

My first thought is, "What a world, oh my goodness, it's a wonder anybody can function in a world that's so unsafe and alarming and everything's going south and nothing's going right and it's all . . . "

That's called a downshift. My beautiful mind coming out of a wonderful dream gets plugged into the "news" and it downshifts. It's just like an automatic transmission when your car mounts a hill.

My mind is always on automatic when I myself am not doing the shifting. Downshifting all the way.

So I change. Now it's on manual. I take a breath. I enter a sacred place. I read a spiritual passage. I listen to inspired music. I breathe. I meditate. I let my thoughts fall away, like the dead, colorful leaves from a tree in the fall. I realize my happiness in life was always already there.

I don't have to listen to all the bombarding, ratings-boosting scare-tactics that come in from the media, because that will always be stress-related and fear-related. That's how the media makes its money. I can always set the stage for a shift above and beyond that level. I can always create my own news.

I am as light as a feather, I am as happy as an angel, I am as merry as a school boy. I am as giddy as a drunken man. A merry Christmas to everybody! A happy New Year to all the world!

Ebenezer Scrooge,
after awakening on Christmas morning,
in *A Christmas Carol* (1843)

~ Charles Dickens

48

The power of numbers on paper

Something comes in the mail, and we open the envelope and take out the piece of paper and read that we owe a precise amount of money, and realize that this is a bill.

This bill is on a piece of paper, and the exact amount of money that we owe has been written on this paper. We treat this bill with tremendous respect. (Mainly because it arrives printed on a piece of paper. It arrives in the mail, and so this is serious reality. This is the real thing!)

I may owe this exact rent payment. Or I may owe this exact mortgage payment. I owe this exact utility payment. If I do not pay the utility payment they will turn off my lights and power and, believe me, I've had that happen! I do *not* want to ignore this piece of paper!

Paper is a very serious thing. Isn't it? Most people spend their whole lives reacting to pieces of paper. Because it's on paper, it's real, and they better find a way to pay attention to it.

Now I set these papers down on my kitchen table. I will look at them again when I come home tonight. I'll look at them again and say, "Yeah, it's serious stuff, it really needs to be paid," and that thought now shapes my life.

It begins to feel like I'm living an outside-in kind of life. I'm simply living up to other people's demands. Isn't that how life now feels? And the problem is that it's a feeling that does not inspire me. It does not lift me up to my most creative and energetic state. Quite the opposite! It pulls me down to that well-worn rung near the bottom.

I know somehow it doesn't have to be like this. It can be a more well-balanced life than this. But what to do? How can I balance the playing field?

The mind shift is here: What if I, too, used the power of paper?

What if I took the time to write my *own* demands and numbers down? What if there were pieces of paper that contained numbers that came from *me?*

If I want to make a certain amount of money, if I want to weigh a certain amount of pounds, if I want to add a certain number of clients this month—those numbers can go on paper!

I will put them on index cards and place them up around my computer. I will put them in the bathroom, and put them up by the mirror. I will go over them every morning and look at them. I will put numbers on them and due dates! I will make them as important as the *other* bills that come in, only these bills serve me! They don't leave me with less money . . . they leave me with more.

I'm not saying anyone *has to* do this. I'm just saying it sure helped me during a time in my life when I felt the walls were closing in. It just occurred to me that not every piece of paper has to reflect a debt I owe. I can put numbers on paper too. I can be the writer and the author of my financial life.

The best way to predict the future
is to create it.

~ **Peter Drucker**

49

The power of your sleeping mind

Any time I am specific enough to use paper, my subconscious helps me achieve things—even when I am not thinking about them. It moves me quickly in the direction of the number I've written down.

I know when I jot down that I want to wake up at six o'clock I open my eyes and it says 5:59 on the clock! Look at how the subconscious works for me that way. When I give it a specific number, picture and timeline, it will move mountains to get things done for me. It knows how to do that. The human biological computer is amazing.

But most people won't program it.

Most people just keep floating vague things into their minds—never putting them on paper, always floating their ideas through the clouds of fantasy: "I want more of this," and "I wish I could have more of that."

It's such a great new practice for me to wake up, take a yellow pad, think about what is it I would like to bring into my life and how specific I can be, and just jot these things down. Now look at them! They are on paper. Which means they've lost their unreality. They've lost their fantasy status. No more fantasy football. This is a real field of play.

For me, without putting new numerical possibilities on paper I will always just automatically (automatic transmission!) keep thinking within the old restricted, narrow paradigm of what I used to do. Maybe I'll be 10 percent better this year. Best case. Even companies do this. How can we increase revenues by 10 percent this year? So the most anyone ever really imagines themselves doing this way is 10 percent better than last year. Which never opens the mind to a new future. It just repeats the past, plus 10 percent. So my future isn't really the future at all! It's the past! (Plus 10 percent.)

The brain is a goal-achieving, bio-computer right here between my ears. Why not use it to create a brand new future?

Creative activity could be described as a
type of learning process where the
teacher and the student are located
in the same individual.

~ **Arthur Koestler**

50

Stop going out of your mind

I only started realizing big mind shifts after I realized that the thoughts I believed were my only real problem.

As I scan books and the internet I notice that success in this world is achieved by millions of people. Therefore there must be a simple process behind it.

I soon realized that if I wanted to succeed at business or at playing the piano or at anything, the process I can follow will be simple and understandable, because people who succeed always leave behind case studies of how they got there.

Hey, I can just follow the simple directions! If everything else fails!

Right now, virtually all the knowledge that anyone has ever had about anything in the whole world is available on the internet. So, if you want to know how to succeed at running a small business, it's right there. If you want to know how to become a better tennis player, it's right there. How to succeed at playing classical piano? It's there—right there! If you follow the logical steps, if you practice regularly, you will succeed.

Yet people think success is filled with intangibles. I know I used to. Mysterious factors. Weirdly superior personality traits. Odd convergences of luck and energy. Not so.

So if it's all so simple (maybe not always easy, but surely simple) why was I not mastering it? And then I saw where it was going wrong. Negative emotions would hijack the place. Fear. Worry. Envy. Resent. Frustration. Discouragement.

And then I would give up and shut down.

How have I let that happen?

What is the source behind this tragic misstep on the path to success?

Finally I got the answer to that. It happens right here: people (like me) believe their emotions have an external cause.

That's it. That's the only real problem. That's the game-stopper. It's a belief, and it's wrong. It's a misunderstanding that almost everybody in the world suffers from, and often "suffers" is too mild a word for it.

People believe their emotions have an external cause! Can you believe it? Do you? Do you see the consequences? Because after that belief is believed, nothing works out.

Once I saw, and then truly SAW that my emotions come from my own personal thoughts, all these outside circumstances and outside people lost their power to frighten or even worry me. I could move in the business world and *create* the circumstances I wanted and *create* the relationships I needed to move forward to success.

No longer just hoping and wishing they would "happen" for me.

No longer afraid of everything and everyone. I could move freely, wake up and create ways to serve people without fearing them. Freedom!

* * *

One of my clients was in an argument with his best customer the other day. He was debating about delivery dates and broken promises, and who said what. Of course, my client was harming his chances of having a good month in his business because of this conversation, but he couldn't see it. He knew he was right. He was taking the argument personally. And he knew he was right!!!

He was emotionally interacting with his number one customer.

If he were logical—if he were simply Mr. Spock on *Star Trek* and did not have the capacity to be upset by this client— everything would have been worked out reasonably. His month's numbers would be just fine and the business would stay on the path to success. But no. He was really ticked off. He felt personally threatened and he converted that to anger and made a real mess of things. All because he believed his bad feelings were coming from this customer.

He'd made the mistake of believing that something outside of him caused him to feel the deep threat he felt.

"Yes, I was upset but that's because my customer backed out of a deal."

Welcome to his world . . . where upset comes not from his thoughts but from the words and actions of others. That will always be a fear-based world for him if there is never a mind shift toward real truth and understanding.

People everywhere are experiencing similar mirages and hallucinations about cause and effect: "Sure I had a bad day but that's because one of my people didn't show up, and another employee said this disloyal thing, and the bank told me our credit wouldn't be as deep anymore."

These people are outsourcing their low feelings. And these are the very feelings that cause them to be ineffective in the face of challenges. But rather than realizing that these are thought-generated feelings, they are pointing their fingers at OUTSIDE CAUSES.

Remember the ladder. When I'm feeling worried, anxious, stressed, nervous, depressed, upset, I'm much less capable of creating good things. I'm not tapping into infinite creativity, and so I'm usually not making any progress toward success.

How could I? How could I maintain clear focus on the simple path to success when I'm likely to be blindsided at any moment? How can I even proceed toward the intersection if there is high likelihood that I'll be tee-boned by another car?

And the longer I stay down there in those dysfunctional states—the less I will achieve.

But when I see it, the mind shifts. I float up the ladder to my natural place at the top (where the human system was designed to dwell). And I realize that, in a strange way, success comes faster when I am allowing myself to recognize and experience that natural state of happiness. Wow. For most of my life I thought happiness would come from success, not the other way around.

* * *

When I visit a company and talk to the salespeople, I will usually notice one salesperson right away on the team who seems happier than the others. I mean, genuinely happy. I don't mean the phony kind of person who looks happy but you can tell they're putting it on. I mean a truly genuine twinkle in the eye.

Later, I find out, not to my surprise, that person is selling more than the other people are.

Maybe you're thinking: "Well, yeah, I'd be happy, too, if I made as much money as he did," but it's the other way around. It's the ability to stay at the happy level that creates and improves the success.

But people low on the ladder always believe that some event can make them feel bad. They can also believe that some other person is responsible for how they now feel.

They don't see they're living in a world of false causes. The problem with false causes is that there can be no solutions. I'm always looking in the wrong direction as I try to fix my life. Of course there will be no solutions.

So, here's the problem. If I believe that my feelings are caused by other people and events, then I'm *always feeling* that

I need to control and defend against other people and events—the very things in life that are blessedly *out* of my control. How confused is that?

I show up for work, something happens and now I'm low. I'm feeling down. So I'm non-productive for a long period of time.

I could turn that around if I realized how the biological computer works. But I will only realize a mind shift if I know that inside the mind all feelings are caused by thoughts. If I think another person is the source I am lost and helpless.

If I stay with this investigation long enough, I will see and realize for myself (and not have to take another person's word for it . . . not have to add on a new cumbersome belief to have to remember to believe in) that my feelings are not caused by anything around me. They are not caused by anything other than thought.

It's *what I think* about what happens that makes me feel the way I do. It's not what happens.

If it's raining outside, one person I know walks to the window and says, "Oh boy, it's raining. How refreshing. How great. We need rain. What a blessing."

But another person walks to the same window and says, "Aaah, look at that, how dreary, bad weather again. Oh, man, this is really a downer."

So, we have the same rain falling. The exact same event and circumstance! But two different people are walking away from the window with two completely different feelings about it. If the event were causative, that wouldn't happen. It couldn't happen.

But it isn't causative. Only thought is causative. And one person's thought was negative and the other's positive. Yet each one of the two people believed that the rain itself *made them feel* a certain way. They both saw rain as cause.

But if rain could cause a feeling, they'd both be feeling the same way.

Rain cannot be cause. Rain itself has no meaning. Until I attach a thought to it. And I'm free to attach any thought or not attach any thought. That's my primary and greatest freedom in all of life.

The email I get from my boss has no meaning, until I give it meaning. The competitor moving in across the street means nothing, until I give it meaning. The downturn in the market means nothing, until I create a meaning around it, and so, therefore, all these feelings that suffocate, drown and smother my creative energy and thereby go against my success have been caused by my thoughts—not by events.

Events cannot cause feelings—they don't have that power. It's not really how the brain works. The biological computer processes thoughts. So when something happens, I have to *think* it's a threat in order to be scared.

Some people love snakes. I mean really, truly love them so they see a snake in the yard and they go softly, slowly toward the snake. If they see it's a garter snake, they love it, they pick it up, they're charmed. The snake has made their day.

Another person sees a snake in the yard and goes running inside, heart pounding. How creepy, oh my goodness.

Now which is it? Which feeling does poor Mr. Snake cause in people? Neither. He is not cause.

* * *

When I work with clients who I can tell are in creatively suppressed states about something (in other words they are worried about it or they're scared about it or they are angry about it), I want to find the *thought* that creates that feeling.

Because once we can challenge and evaporate that thought, they're free now to create success. The formula for business success is logical and understandable. It really is. You can sit down with a business—a small business that's not succeeding—and you can figure out why.

If you are a consultant, you can see what's keeping the business from succeeding. You can see what needs to be done.

But often the owners themselves can't see it because they are *believing all these scary thoughts* about false causes, and they're going into these profoundly dysfunctional, irrational behaviors throughout the day. That's what's leading to their failure. Soon failure brings more failure, and these bad feelings bring more bad results and so they seem to confirm themselves as apparently true. Beliefs about impending doom almost always seem to make themselves come true! ("We could lose everything!")

When I work with clients who are in this state I want to ask, "What is it that you're *thinking* about this situation?"

"Well the competitor just moved in—it could be the end of us."

"Well, let's look at that. What's the thought about the competitor that you're thinking that causes you to feel all this fear? Let's look at it."

"They're going to take all my business away."

"Is that really true? Let's think that through. Let's say the competitor runs a lot of advertising and wakes the whole community up to how great this product is that you both sell. And now there's a spill-over effect to your business because the competitor has run radio ads and done door hangers and everybody's now awake to how great this product can be, and people notice you are across the street so they check both of you out, and your sales go up. Now wouldn't that just as likely happen? And what if your customer service was so much better than the competitor's that any time anyone comparison-shopped they would end up with you. So now the competitor has done nothing but stimulate interest in *you,* without you paying for any of that advertising."

By the way, this often really does happen. There's a successful business, and because it's successful somebody else thinks well, we could do that too, and they come into the location and they try to do the same thing and they spend a lot of early money on marketing. They raise the awareness of the general service and the product, because they don't really know how to be specific enough yet, they are not that skilled in direct marketing, and so their rising tide lifts all boats and soon there's more traffic at your store than there's ever been.

And yet most people, when they hear about competition, get scared, and they get upset and they fret and they do crazy, self-destructive things based on fear. They don't work very well with existing customers now because their mind is into a *projected future* in which they could lose everything.

"We could lose it all!"

But it's the thought "I could lose everything" that makes me more likely to lose everything. Because of what it does to my energy and creativity.

If I could see that it's always my thought that gets in the way and makes me scared, I would experience a mind shift. I would take a breath and fall out of that thinking and return to inner peace. I might even notice an elevation of my thinking back up to the creatively strategic level—the logical systems level.

This is not some kind of dreamy, new age concept applied to business. Even the hardest core manufacturing expert W. Edwards Deming said the most *practical* first mandatory step in transforming the productivity of a business was to "eliminate fear" from the people working there.

There are certain things you can only know by creating them for yourself.

~ **Werner Erhard**

51

You can have a secret advantage

Once you've decided you want to succeed at something, one of the things I recommend very strongly is to look for a way that you can give yourself a hidden advantage. Something other people don't have that you have.

When I started doing public speaking, I used to talk to other speakers and hear them say, "What do you do when your voice goes hoarse? That's such a problem for me. I give three seminars in three days and my voice is shot at the end, and it's embarrassing. It's hard to be powerful when you can barely speak."

I decided that wouldn't happen with me.

Those same public speakers would also say, "What do you do when the microphone goes out, or the audio system breaks down and you're there in front of 400 people in the hall . . . What do you do?"

I decided that, too, would never be a problem.

I noticed that all these public speakers would have so many horror stories about how hard it is to be a public speaker because of how many things that can go wrong with the system or your voice.

I even have a colleague today who still tells me, "I'm about to do one of my four-day marathon seminars and boy it always gets rough right around the second day . . . I lose my voice, and here I'm drinking cough syrup and gargling and doing all these tricks, but it's pretty ragged."

Well, I decided early on I wasn't going to have that happen. After experimenting with it I realized that if I would sing an hour a day, on the average, that I would never have a problem with my voice, and that I could always fill the auditorium with it, even if the AV system went down and the microphone went out. The voice would be strong enough to fill the room. Today I can speak to a hall with 900 people in it without a microphone and the people in the back of the room can hear me.

"You've been blessed with quite a voice," some people tell me. Not true. But if they want to believe it's true I let them. Actually, before I started my singing practice, I didn't have much of a voice at all.

We often mislabel someone's long-practiced capability as "talent." It's easier that way. You can work six hours a day for a year on a book and people will say, "You have such a natural talent for writing. It's a gift."

People say, "I wish I was like that, and I wish I could do that . . . I wish . . . I wish . . . I wish."

They don't know that most of these "talents" have been *created*, and that all these people *could* do these things! Yet they prefer to admire from afar with clasped hands pressed to their chests and eyes dreamy with envy.

Ever since I decided I would sing an hour a day I've found a way to work it in. If I had to drive to do an errand, I would bring CD's that I could sing with, and often I would drive around a lot before and after the errand to get the hour in.

"What took you so long?" my business partner asks.

I'd often bring CD's that were a stretch for me, out of my range, beyond my levels, so I'd always be strengthening and stretching. Because if I just sing along with Johnny Cash all day not much is going to happen.

When I tell other speakers that I do that they look at me like I'm crazy or obsessed. Yet if you speak for a living, your voice is your primary tool. Would we call a woodcutter obsessed for sharpening his saw each day? Is he a madman? Wouldn't we want our favorite third baseman to take batting practice? Would we call him obsessed if he took a little extra practice during (or before!) a slump?

There's a false story about talent that can be shifted in the mind.

"Michael Jordan, though! He was *born* with it. If I had been born with that athleticism, I would have been a basketball star, too."

People really believe these things. So no wonder their world is bereft of opportunity. They live in a world of false limitation, with a mind that never shifts. They believe forces beyond their control are responsible for success. But that's the most counter-productive belief anyone could ever have. People are doomed from the start if they believe that.

Michael Jordan was cut from his high school basketball team. So much for innate, natural, inborn talent being all you need.

After that experience, Michael Jordan practiced more than anyone else did. But no one wants to hear about that. Because it would bring them back into the gym.

Their thoughts think of that and reject it. But if they just went to the gym and allowed themselves to enjoy themselves, great things would happen.

The body says what words cannot.

~ **Martha Graham**

52

Your body can lead the way

Your lungs can fuel the journey. Your brain can thrive on oxygen.

The physical nature of life is so important! It affects how I think, how I feel, my mood, my impulse to creativity. Quite often I can elevate my mood just by getting up and walking around. If I'm sitting at my computer and I'm locked into a problem I can't solve, I'll just walk around and take some deep breaths. That will elevate my mood. Shift me up the ladder.

If I work visits to the gym and health club into my week and actually put them on the calendar so they can't be moved, that will *increase* my energy (even though it seems like it would do the opposite. That's thought for you.)

People think working out would be a great expenditure of time and energy. But what it really does is *open up* energy and time. It allows me to think faster and do things with a clearer mind.

So I want to create a physical equivalent for whatever it is that I'm achieving—so I don't leave that out. I want to always see that it's mind, body and spirit, and not necessarily in that order. If the spirit is low I can turn to the body. If the mind is low—I can't solve a problem that is bothering me—I can actually lift the mind by taking a long walk, or taking a run or going for a swim—or even singing!

Singing is just one physical act that draws oxygen in and makes the blood stream richer and opens up the lungs and brain so I can think more clearly and get intuitions I didn't have before. When I breathe in, I'm inspired—that's what inspiration means. *Res*piration—*in*spiration, and I'm breathing into the spirit in me that was born to succeed. It was born to have fun and be fulfilled.

It's as much in you as it is in me.

A nail is driven out by another nail.
Habit is overcome by habit.

~ **Desiderius Erasmus**

53

Stop trying to break habits

My client Mickey said, "I know I've got to try to break this habit."

He wanted to oppose his habit, and be angry at it, and take a stand against it, and then break it into pieces.

The problem with that, Mick, is that it will push back. It will persist *because* you are fighting it and trying to break it. It will grow even stronger in significance because you've created inner conflict with it. You're feeding it with your resistance.

Also, on some strange but true level your ego believes it *needs* that habit. A habit always has some subconscious "survival" value for you so it's going to try to maintain itself if you try to force it out of your life.

So don't fight it. Replace it. Replace it with an upgraded, healthier look-alike. Habits cannot be broken, but they *can* be replaced and that's really the approach that works for me and the people I work with.

Let's look back on my life as an example. I was stuck in the habit of addiction to alcohol use for years. It was a horrific habit. It was a terrible addiction, life-threatening, life-destroying—all the things you've read and heard about if you haven't been through it yourself.

So, I could try to fight it off and just use willpower and go on a dry drunk and white-knuckle it through the rest of my life, fighting off the temptation to drink every time I went out to a social occasion or suffered an emotional story. But that's been proven not to work so well.

What does work is to replace the habit—not break it. What works—better than medication, better than psychology—is a spiritual program of recovery. That has the best track record and there's a reason for that.

When a person works a spiritual program of recovery from an addiction, they're actually *replacing* false spirit with true spirit. They're not just eliminating alcohol and going back to zero. They are replacing the "freedom" that they thought alcohol gave them, or the "release" it gave them, with something similar but better.

It's interesting that in the Old West, alcohol was described as "spirits." It's also interesting that alcohol was referred to as "false courage."

In a good program of recovery, alcohol gets replaced with true spirit and the courage to change the things you can. You are blessed with the serenity to accept the things you cannot change. Spiritual progress is now happening in life as opposed to the false chemical spirit you were pouring into an anxious human body.

The problem with addictive drugs and alcohol is that they always eventually backfire. They turn against you. What they were intended to do turns back around and goes at you. Stephen King couldn't have invented a greater horror. (But maybe *The Shining* was his attempt. For "Johnny" had a bit of a drinking problem, didn't he?)

My good friend Lindsay Brady is a hypnotherapist with a great track record for helping people quit smoking. He gets great results in just one visit.

He replaces a person's self-concept on the matter of smoking. They go into his office perceiving themselves to be a smoker and after the session, they walk out with a new self-concept, a new self-perception that says, "I am a non-smoker." And as a non-smoker they naturally build healthy lungs with deep breathing; their health becomes vibrant, it increases, and they get better feelings about life because of the way they can breathe now as a non-smoker.

Non-smokers don't smoke.

So it's not just "quitting smoking" that's going on—smoking is being perceptually replaced by something that's even better, and that's really the way to get rid of a habit.

If I have a habit, for example, of having a messy workspace I might decide that I don't want that—I want more organization. Then what I can do is *replace* the messy workspace with something that I like better and that functions better. I don't just want to get rid of the mess. I don't want to just break the habit of being disorganized, I want to create a new system that I actually like better. Otherwise there's no replacement. It won't hold. Ever.

So always look for something you can replace your habit with that's better. Because subconsciously your habit is there as a survival mechanism. At some level you think that this habit is something you need. So in order for that subconscious clinging to the habit to be let go, you want to show your subconscious mind that the new system you've introduced into your life is even better! Then it can let go.

That's the law of creation. Create a replacement for the habit you don't like. Do not react to the habit by fighting it off. The law of creation is a law that can kick in at any stage when you're ready to allow a mind shift.

Many people die with their music still in them. Why is this so? Too often it is because they are always *getting ready* to live. Before they know it, time runs out.

~ Oliver Wendell Holmes

54

Today will always be my big day

I love waking up to those two choices I have. I can *get* ready to live, or I can live right now.

This getting ready to live is often a misinterpretation of the goal-setting process that we talked about earlier. It's beautiful to have goals when you love them and allow them to inspire you. It's wonderful to have projects; but I don't want them to be an excuse for me to try to live in the future.

There's a way to have a precise goal and still live in the present moment. Think of the goal only as a map. If I have a map and I'm going somewhere, I don't want to stare at the map while I'm driving. I want to enjoy the trip. The reason I even have the map is so that I have confidence that I know where I'm going, so I can enjoy the trip along the way.

So the map is good. There's nothing worse than trying to get somewhere without an address or map. But once I've looked at that map, I want to set it aside and enjoy the journey. Because if I'm always staring at the map (obsessed with the future) all my thoughts are in the future, and now the trip itself is no good. I'm even more likely to get in an accident or fall off the cliff staring at my phone's map.

This is also true when I'm projecting—*what if something bad happens?* Or I'm thinking, *I'll be happy when certain conditions are met.* I'm going to be miserable in the present because I'm not here. I'm not here for myself.

So a real strong point here on the road to success, is get out of the future. Byron Katie says if you want to be miserable, get yourself a future. She's trying to shake people awake with that statement. She means that if you are living in your own future, if you're holding your happiness hostage to some future condition, the present moment is full of anxiety—you cannot enjoy it.

So I want to bring life back to the present moment. Exactly what the great basketball coach, John Wooden, was talking about. When he said, "Make each day your masterpiece."

So have *today* be the day! It all happens today! My future is today. This transforms everything, including, ironically, the future itself. Because the future is created in the present moment. It's what you're doing now that creates your future.

This is a valued mind shift. Back into the present moment. Shifting out of where I have spent most of my non-productive life. In the future, like this:

"I'm working toward the day when I can . . . "

"I'm hoping to be able to . . . and maybe someday I can . . . "

I was putting my whole happiness out into the future in some futuristic, fantasy moment and it never came. When I keep pushing my fulfillment, my financial security and happiness into the future, the very *pushing of it* into the future develops a neurological pathway in the brain that becomes a groove and a rut. It becomes an automatic, knee-jerk, habitual way of thinking. So even when I arrived at the situation that I used to think would make me happy, my mind-groove now pushes happiness into the future again. Automatically. Out of habit. Always in the future. Arrive-push, arrive-push!

"Well, when I get a *second* house . . . when we've got a second home, that's when I'll really be happy. When I have a boat. I know I said that I'd be happy when I have this car, I know I said that, but I didn't really understand it, because what I didn't see was that we don't have a boat and you know really,

really, to be really happy, you need to have your own boat, I would think . . . that's what I imagine anyway. A boat! Being able to go out on the water. Not rent one, but own one."

Insanity. An endless, insane addition of material possessions and emotional conditions that I imagine would bring happiness in the future. If you want to be miserable get yourself a future. If you want to be happy, get yourself this day today.

The question isn't who is going to let me; it's who is going to stop me.

~ **Ayn Rand**

55

Selling in this vital present moment

In my sales training days I would often go on a call with a sales person I was training. I'd sit with them while they talked to their prospective customers. I noticed that the creative sales people would find opportunity in anything. Even in objections! Even in a client saying, "We don't have a budget this coming quarter; we're not going to be doing much with you."

A good salesperson would use that information to generate an even stronger, more committed agreement with the client . . . mapping out a creative payment plan that adjusted to the budget flux.

But most sales people were always mentally *hurling* themselves into the future. So when they heard the client say, "There's no budget right now," they would think, "Oh no, oh no, no, no. Oh shoot, no budget? Oh well, well, OK, I'll talk to you next quarter then. Wow, that was bad news. I don't know what I'll tell my wife tonight."

They developed an inability to see the opportunity in the moment by always worrying about (living in) in the future.

The masterful sales person sits in the present moment. Allowing the gentle inquiry of service to arise: "What can help this person?" They are always focused on the well-being of the end user, not their own commission.

They might say, "Well, you don't have a budget this quarter,

I understand that. Let's look at how we can still help you get what you want, and see what we can do for you, so we serve you anyway. There might be a payment plan for you."

There are so many hidden opportunities in what people say. But if my mind is in the future, I will never hear any of them. I'll just say goodbye to wealth, say goodbye to that person, and we will both walk away, and that will be the end of it.

But when I am right here, right now, nowhere else to go, nowhere else to be, the only thing I will care about right now is serving *you* and contributing to *you*; and so then I can hear so many things in what you say to me. I can hear so many opportunities for service. Our relationship can get even better inside "no opportunity."

Living in the past doesn't work well, either. So many people waste all their precious mental treasure and energy focused on the past. Trying to revisit all the hurts and disappointments. They think it helps them understand themselves better. In truth it keeps them out of the present-moment opportunity.

An interesting related email today came from my friend Dr. Carla Rotering, a truly visionary physician. She said:

> I was thinking of my ex-husband last night, who spends his life as a paleontologist sifting through rubble for some meaningful relic that will help him create a story of the earth of the past as a way of predicting the earth of the future. I thought of the thousands of fossils he has found, and about the famous dinosaur he excavated (my son Josh has a tattoo of it on his chest), all kept shielded behind glass so that we might never touch or feel them. So it goes for most of us, perhaps . . . that ceaseless sorting through the stones and rocks we call our history so that we might find some remnant we call true as an explanation (or dispensation!!) of the details of our lives. We put those old relics behind glass, call them precious and untouchable, and allow them to create— from their INERTNESS—the story of what our lives are "meant to be." I believe the past has earned a certain kind of honor. But this isn't a conversation about honoring the past.

It is a conversation about putting that legitimate past to illegitimate use in a way that holds us in a motionless and false sense of helplessness. Or, at least, it does that for me.

Oh it's not just you, Carla. It's all of us. Even those of us who are looking so successful on TV playing professional golf.

One of the things that other golfers say is different about Tiger Woods is that when he steps over the ball with the club, all he thinks about is putting a good swing on *this ball*, right now, right here. Just this one swing and just this one ball, right now.

Whereas, most of the other golfers are fretting and thinking about the past and the future. They're still carrying that last bad hole (that old relic) in their mind, and hating themselves, and wondering how they're going to make up for that blunder with a better hole this time: "Do I have to take more risks now to get ahead?" Or, they're thinking about the future: "I'm feeling a little fatigued, and what about that next hole after this? How will I feel then?" Their mind is all over the place.

Meanwhile Tiger Woods has created an ability—a skill developed through practice—to shift his mind's focus off of all that. He shifts his mind from the past to the present. He shifts his mind from the future to the present. And once shifted and relaxed into place, he just puts a swing on the ball.

There are two points of view. Both are normal, one is true. From the point of view of a personal or separate self, there are distinct objects, events, and selves. There is isolation; only insecurity. From the point of view of Consciousness itself, there is one indivisible, yet perpetually changing experience. There is freedom; only Love.

~ Garret Kramer

56

How most people get it wrong

When people believe that they have a particular fixed personality it can become a prison for them. What was once formed to give them, perhaps, a hoped-for sense of safety, identity and individuality, now can put them in total lockdown.

When I work with people who want to excel but aren't excelling, one of the first things I see getting in the way is what they believe their fixed personality is. What they believe they are like, and therefore must always be like.

Now it's true that people have various belief systems inside themselves that have been created from childhood by repeated thoughts. These systems become what everyone else calls "personality," but it's anything but fixed.

There's nothing permanent in them, or anything else out in the physical world under the sun.

Yet people's imaginary permanent characteristics can become like a religion to them. Something to believe in! They might have been indoctrinated into the dogma early: they were told they were lazy, or disorganized, or cowardly, or that they weren't thoughtful about other people. Soon these various personality characteristics became their beliefs.

Who among us can really see that they are only fleeting *thoughts?* Very few do, but everyone can!

Once again, let's use the example of the house burning down

across the street. I run out of my house and I hear a small child crying inside the flames and I run in, I grab the child and I bring her out. All of this was done in a heightened state of *action beyond and without personal thought*. I was swept up in and then carried by what I felt simply needed to be done. It almost felt automatic. No time to think! Just did it! So it certainly wasn't the result of any particular personality showing its stuff.

We read accounts of a grandmother lifting the back of a car to free a trapped child or animal. Incredible feats of courage and improbable strength.

But we can't see that it comes from dropping the illusion of a permanent personality and allowing the fertile void to replace it with immediate action. A noun drops away to get replaced by a verb.

Your restrictive, permanent personality was never anything but repeated thoughts. They were repeated enough times to make a made-up illusion of "you," just the way a sparkler at night waved in a circle looks like a glowing whole circle. It's not a thing! It's a rotation of disappearing light. That's who the personal "you" are.

In the moment of *now* you can drop all of that rotating thought you call you. You can be whoever you choose to be given the higher purpose calling to you. You can have your actions called *forth by* the game you are playing, instead of trying to *come out of* your personality. Such good news for those (including the old me) hung up inside pathological limitation.

We are what we pretend to be,
so we must be careful
about what we pretend to be.

~ Kurt Vonnegut

57

Stop trying to decide whether to…

When your life is on a roll do you ever notice how decision-making can stop the whole thing? How it throws a monkey wrench into your creative flow?

When I see people who are really stuck, they're usually trying to decide something.

"I'm trying to decide whether to leave my husband."

"I'm trying to decide whether to take this job."

"I'm trying to decide whether to do this report this afternoon or go to that meeting."

And you can notice physically that these people are really out of sorts. They're really stressing out inside feeling stuck.

The beauty of being on the wing and in flight, and in motion, is that no "decision" ever needs to be made in that state of mind. The "decision" makes itself while you are in motion.

You can watch this on the football field.

You see players calling a time out. The camera shows us the sideline where the coach's face is twisted and his head is jerking around like an agitated insect's while he's listening on the headphones. Why does he look like he's in so much pain?

He's trying to make a decision.

He's trying to decide which play to run. Indecisiveness is hard to watch. So we're almost glad to go to commercial.

So now out on the field that play is finally being run, but

something goes wrong. The defense has foiled the play! So now the quarterback spins and runs out in the other direction. His receivers now come back to the quarterback to try to help him out (they have already run their routes!). The quarterback is now just *on the run*, he's on the move and BOOM!!!!! he hits a receiver with a pass. The receiver turns upfield, and runs through a confused defense . . . look at that receiver now! He just may go all the way!

Let's learn something from that great play. The quarterback says in the postgame interview that he didn't ever really "decide" who to throw the ball to. The ball just flew out of his hand. Almost by itself. There wasn't time to over-think it with a 330-pound guy about to flatten him. An opening appeared, a pass happened and the receiver caught it and went upfield!

These wonderful, unexpected moments happen all the time in sports.

When people do great things like that they describe it as happening almost by itself. An opening appears and something happens before you can think about it. People later say weird things like, "It came through me. I didn't decide to do it, it moved through me."

It will move through you, too, if "you" get out of its way.

Being in action opens the mind for such a shift. It allows intuition to decide things for you. It has you trusting your wisdom and not wasting time and energy "trying to decide" things.

Fortune sides with the
person who dares.

~ **Virgil**

58

Converting your energy into money

How do I convert my inner wisdom into prosperity?

The first shift is to create a warm and relaxed relationship with prosperity. The very thought of it. I want to visualize the people my prosperity will help—including me and my family. I'm a person. I count as part of the category known as "people" whenever I think the words, "I want to help people."

Contrast that world-friendly mindset to the thought-produced condition that we usually fasten to like tree toads: I am angry about my standard of living, and fearful about money, clinging to every little bit of loose change I have, and I'm resentful! Mad at the government, and wondering which program is going to take care of me, and how come my health care can't be free, and how come this, and how come that. It's just a mass of worry and resentment around everything that has to do with money.

Those money fears now produce my absurd fear of failure. I'm not realizing that I fail because I fear failure . . . and if I didn't indulge that fear (or believe that it's really terrifying to fail at something) I would find the freedom to dare more things. To dare and then dare again. Thereby getting fortune on my side.

If the things I believe about money make me afraid, then I want to usher those things out. But how?

There are two ways that have worked for me. One is to get a coach. If you are serious about succeeding, I recommend having a coach or a mentor of some kind. Just as every athlete does, every actor does, everybody who really wants to succeed does. Athletes and actors can't afford to just get by or be mediocre. They must be *really good* to even remain in their profession! Therefore they all get coaches. Want to be really good at something? Get a coach. Always. No exceptions. Even Jordan Spieth has a coach.

Find a life coach, or a business coach, and keep looking until you find one you really love, and who really resonates with you.

Find someone who will help you allow the fear of money to drop out, and put those fears out there for your coach to be aware of so (s)he can see them for what they are.

If you don't want to do that or don't have the money to do that yet, I recommend you go to Byron Katie's website, and go to her books, because she's got such a great process for questioning limiting, fear-based beliefs.

Or go to Pransky & Associates and let George Pransky and his team of masterful counselors help you understand how humans really function in the world . . . how thought works, and why consciousness and the divine universal mind have your back.

So those are the two things I would immediately do once you have identified fear as a possible speed bump on the way to true prosperity.

Now that the fear is gone, or at least seen for what it is, let's move. Rather than just pining away for a "better" job that suits your calling better, the real ascendance can happen immediately when you throw your heart into this job right here. That's how you rise up. Only after rising up can you see more. The better you do at any one thing, the more possibilities open to you. The higher you rise, the more you can see. It's a law of the universe. Then you just keep going higher.

Most people mentally "stuck" and discouraged in their current work are victims of their own thinking. But spiritual insight and inspired action are the answer to this. This learning curve you've put yourself on keeps you evolving into things you love even more.

In today's global market, with all the leverage that the internet gives you to reach out to the world instantly, it's much easier to find what you love to do and tap into it than it ever was before. A lot of people I know now are writing books. They would never have dreamed of writing books before, because in the past (not too distant past) if you wrote a book, you had to find a publisher to approve of and "accept" your work. Otherwise, your book would never be in any bookstores and so people would not have a chance of reading your book. Shelf space was everything.

But today you can skip all those steps. You can publish your own book, and people can buy it off your website. You can put it on Amazon after you have published it yourself, and people buy it not knowing, or caring, whether your book has been published by a major publisher or is self-published. A lot of authors today who have had books published by major publishers also self-publish some of their books, and their readers don't know which is which, or care. Who cares? If a book is good why do I care where it was published?

The same goes for music, or blogs or any other product or service you create.

There's an old saying that actually rings true: "Do what you love, and the money will follow." People love to pay for things that are lovingly created, and joyfully delivered. They don't like paying for things that are reluctantly delivered, with poor work behind them.

So even if you aren't doing the one true calling you would love . . . love what you *are* doing. Start there.

To succeed, we must embrace the linking of love, service and wealth together. We must be enlightened enough to see it because the global marketplace is fertile enough to receive it. Love, service, wealth. Love, service, wealth. If I can get that pattern going—get that rhythm happening—I'll get that syncopation going in my mind. What do I love to do for people? How can I serve more people with it? And wealth will come as a result of that.

In the past, it was different. In the very near past it was duty, it was obligation, it was figuring out a way to win approval so that you could earn a living. It was winning a position somewhere, and it was all a struggle because it was all about manipulating, and playing politics, winning people over and playing the corporate game. All those old-style, hierarchal structures of companies based on the old monarchical systems where there are superior humans and subservient humans are no longer sustained.

Now that whole paradigm is being dissolved by a simple mind shift. Individuals can now simply choose to do what they love, then sell it, and make their money.

Work is love made visible. And if you cannot work with love but only with distaste, it is better that you should leave your work and sit at the gate of the temple and take alms of those who work with joy.

~ Khalil Gibran

59

You can be efficient and effective

I was talking to a good friend the other day. He's a public speaker and a trainer. I asked him how his day was going and he said he had just spent a couple hours doing something he really hated to do.

I asked what that was and he said, "I was gathering all my receipts from my recent trip—all these little cab driver receipts and little scraps of crumpled paper, and I was typing up an expense report. I am going to send it to the client so I can be reimbursed."

I said, "Okay, well, how much does that make you? If you spend two hours on that—what's your return on that?"

And he said, "Well it's almost nothing, I don't really make anything. What it does is it sort of balances things out. What I've already paid out in expenses, so I really make nothing."

"So why do you do that? Why do you spend two hours of your time (your precious time), when you are a very creative individual? You bill your time out at a very high fee, and yet here are two hours being spent where almost nothing comes back."

He stopped and thought. He didn't realize that he was doing that. He always assumed he had to file his own receipts. But a work-at-home bookkeeper could handle all of it for him for less than 5 percent of what he could make in those two hours if they were spent on high-return creative activity rather than low-return busy work.

There are many options that open themselves to you once you commit to a business life of high-return. You can raise your fee so that the client just pays a single fee covering all expenses. So you don't have to do a second billing for expenses. That's the way I do it. It's much simpler. The clients even like it better.

I knew a husband and wife team that had an architectural firm. They made a great deal of money. They were very bright. They were wonderful architects. They worked on the east coast in a seaside community city where they had built their own little business up from nothing.

But they couldn't shake their money fear and the irrational behavior that it caused. So on the weekends they would both go in and clean their office and vacuum and dust. They did all the cleaning of the office themselves. To "save money."

And so I said, "Is that something you just love? Is that your ideal scene for enjoying the weekend? Do you do it as a kind of Zen meditation?"

They said, "No, it's just that it's a way to save some money."

I had to scratch my head, and I said, "My goodness, how much do you really save by doing that yourself."

"Oh, these cleaning firms cost a lot."

Money fear had knocked their thoughts out of proportion.

I tried to explain it to them. To free them up.

Let's say you decide to work four hours on a weekend. Nothing wrong with that if you want to. What if—instead of cleaning your office for those four hours you made it a point to meet with a major client every Saturday morning, serve them breakfast in the office, and review past and future projects?

If they did that, they could move their business forward, financially, in a really major way, instead of saving a couple hundred dollars. They could open themselves up to the possibility of millions in the future by creating deeper and more collaborative relationships with their clients.

After two weekends of trying this they were delighted by the positive results for their business. (It's called high-return activity.) Most people aren't even aware of the difference . . . or how many hours they waste in low-return, hypnotic, automatic work.

As I look at my last week's activities, I might see that I wasted a lot of hours answering email. Ding-ding, here's another email, I'll answer it . . . I'll answer it . . . answering email, taking phone calls, doing this, doing that—I waste so much time when I don't see it.

Here's what's really amazing. If for some medical reason I had been forced to work only half days last week, I would have been *more* productive—not less. Because that would have woken me up to efficiency. It would have made time precious.

Notice what happens when you go on a vacation. The day before you go on vacation, you get so much done. You get about three days' work done in one day! Why? Because the 80/20 rule kicks in. You now know that you are going to be gone for two weeks, so you have to do only the most important things. The 20 percent of actions that bring you 80 percent of your results.

Those other little things that usually take all your time? You just delegate those out.

"Will you do this call for me? I'm going to be gone."

To become wealthy the trick is delegate those things out *now*, so every day is the day before vacation.

Shift from being busy with the trivial to being focused on your most important work. Now what happens when you make that mind shift? The world shifts in response. The world is like your shadow on a sunny day. Make your move and see what the shadow does. It will always move with you! The world out there is the same.

Life is not a problem to be solved,
but a reality to be experienced.

~ Søren Kierkegaard

60

Shifting out of the unreal

One of the most important ways to shift the mind on our way to success is to shift from what's unreal to what's real. When you are working with what's really *real* you can get to success so much faster.

Imagine you are walking down the narrow road toward home, and there's a boulder in the road and you see it and say "I've got to take a side road now—I've got to do something different—I've got to go through the woods to get to my home, because there's a boulder in the road."

Now you're in the woods plowing through the thicket, trying to find an opening to get back home—to success, to wherever you want to go in life.

But what if that boulder in the road were not real? What if the boulder was just an illusion—something you thought was real—it looked real—everyone said it was real—and because you *believed* it was real, you are in the woods, pushing through the poison ivy, the poison oak, trying to get back home?

Absurd example? Well it happens every day. We are sidetracked by imaginary fears every day. That's why reality is so important to work with.

Because the real road to success is often so clear we can't see it.

So we stop and take side roads, and soon that's called "being busy" or "fighting fires" or handling big problems. Most people do this. They are overwhelmed by their distractions. They become too busy to succeed.

What if, instead of busy, I were "focused" in a relaxed, but paradoxically, energetic way. Focused, locked in, excited, enthusiastic, one-pointed.

I got a call the other day from a person who was apologizing to me for missing a phone appointment he had with me.

He said, "I'm sure you understand that a person like me, running businesses that I run, is very busy all the time and I'm so sorry. This time of year it's very busy and I'm sorry I missed the call. You probably run into that a lot, and you're probably even more busy than I am."

I said to him, "No, I am not busy."

And he was stunned, and he waited a minute and said, "What do you mean by that?"

I said, "Busyness for me used to be my story. But it was a surrender to all the things that seemed to call to me throughout the day. It was a cowardly white flag of surrender. I was throwing down my weapons and saying 'OK, take me! Take me in, put me behind bars, torture me!' I was allowing every single thing that called to me to take me away from what it is I really wanted to do. And yet I called it being busy."

I explained how one hour of uninterrupted time is worth any two other hours during my day. I shifted in my mind with this realization: When I'm *selecting* the things I'm going to focus on today, deliberately, based on the road I want to be on, then I can say *no* a lot more easily. I'm more relaxed saying no. Because I have already chosen something else.

When I say yes to what it is I have chosen to do, *no* comes easily. When something comes up or puts its head in the door and says "Got a minute?" I can easily say "No, I don't now," instead of what I used to say. What did I used to say when interruption poked in?

"Okay! Yeah, yeah, sure, sure come on in. Have a seat. What

is it? What's going on?"

"Well, I'm kind of upset with Sally. She said she would do this report . . . but it's like before, she has no respect for my department . . ." and pretty soon my whole life was pulled into the gratuitous drama of other people's victim stories . . . boulders on the road, all false.

The road was actually clear. There was a clear reality-based path to success all along.

Self-concept is destiny.

~ **Nathaniel Branden**

61

Where does my self-concept come in?

If I can see myself doing something based on my self-concept, then my likelihood of doing it is almost guaranteed. It's a very logical thing. It's not some kind of new age concept about self-esteem and self-aggrandizement. It's how the human mind works, and it has everything to do with success.

And by "self"-concept I don't mean the small egoic personality self. My self-concept can be "love and service in action!"

Let's say my self-concept is profound service. From that energy I can see myself easily talking to a "powerful" person . . . the new CEO of a large company I'd love to do business with. I'm in his building and I see him in the lobby and so I immediately strike up a conversation. It was very easy to do, because my self-concept was such that I could see myself engaging him and having him become interested in my work. So it isn't long before he and I are talking.

But what if my self-concept had been different? What if I'd seen myself as my small-self personality, socially inept around big business executives? Then I'd have just watched him in the lobby, not revealing who I was. I wouldn't have approached him because I wouldn't have been able to picture that.

We hardly ever do what *we can't picture ourselves doing.* It's nearly impossible to do it. We only do what we instantaneously picture ourselves being able to do.

So, for example, the reason I don't jump out of this window and fly is because I can't picture it working. I can only picture myself plummeting down to the earth and injuring myself, if not killing myself. That's because my self-concept is such that I'm a human being without wings or any ability to fly. So I stay in the building. And when I leave, I leave by the stairs to the ground floor. Self-concept is destiny.

So whoever I am—to me—drives *what I do* throughout the day. Therefore, if I want to be able to do bigger and better things, then I want to start with my self-concept. It's how I see myself. I need to enlarge it if I want to enlarge the results I'm getting in the world.

That's the next mind shift.

In one of my mastermind meetings, my good friend Lindsay Brady came in. Lindsay is a hypnotherapist, who wrote a wonderful book about hypnosis and what it really is. He calls it perception. As he explained to our group (and dramatically demonstrated through intriguing mental exercises we all did), when the mind sends the brain a picture, the body responds with the appropriate action to get a result.

Any picture my mind sends my brain of who I am and what I am committed to doing, I will do. When there's an opportunity to do that thing I've pictured, I will just move right in and do it, and it will feel natural for me. Self-concept is destiny.

So it's time to pay attention to my self-concept, and not let it contract into a permanent, small person. I want to allow it to continuously expand into the infinite creativity of the universe.

Here's one way that has helped me and many others. Whenever you do something that results in a successful outcome, log it into a file called Who I Am.

Let's say you have a great client conversation. Or you send

an email that gets someone to purchase a large training program—anything that has a good result, you anchor it! You have that be *who you are*. Save the picture of it as the *real you* because, really, you did do it! So it's not some pretend thing that you have to convince yourself of . . . or that you have to *try to believe* in. It's reality. It's certainty. It takes you out of the fear-based world of "trying to believe" or "dying to believe."

If this is new to you, keep a journal. Write down all the things you do that were really successful and productive, so that you can focus on those before you start your tasks. It's the real you, based on reality, not some frantic affirmation that's based on who you are trying to become. The problem with those future-craving affirmations is that because they are really just wishes, they only serve to remind you of who you are not.

To strengthen your self-concept it's important to keep noticing that you *already are* who you need to be. That's the only productive starting point there can ever be.

Review your journal before you start a conversation with someone that you want a result to come from. If you're in sales (and who isn't?) and you're going to have a conversation with someone that you could sell something to that would have a big, good financial result for you, take a moment before the call to refresh and reboot in your own mind who you really are. Profound service and loving kindness. You'll feel a shift from fear to reality.

Why just wander into that call feeling contracted, small, personal, blind and vulnerable? Most people do that! "Here goes nothing!" But why do you want to do that? Do you want to carry in some lingering negative feeling from a bad event that happened a few minutes ago . . . an event that had you feeling down on yourself? If you see yourself in this moment as a rather incompetent, depressed person, you are not going to make much of a connection. Your own self-esteem is always the first thing other people pick up on.

Find the feeling of service in yourself. Find the love of your work and the love of others. Before every call. Shift by rehearsing. Go over the flowing, creative energy that you really are! Is that an artificial manipulation of the mind? No, it's reality-based. It's more real than being vulnerable and weak is.

It's no more artificial than a pianist who rehearses prior to the concert. No one denigrates the pianist and says, "Well, if you have to rehearse—it must not be natural for you to play the piano." Everyone admires the pianist for rehearsing. She has put in hours at the piano so that when she plays for us in concert, it's a beautiful thing. Wow, it sounds so natural, and real, and wonderful, and spontaneous, and expressive, and emotional! Right through her hands to the keys. (It's been rehearsed. Again and again and again.)

I remember when I first started giving speeches my self-concept was not good. I would think, "I don't know how I am going to come across. I don't know what they're going to think of *me*. I better stay in a safe territory and talk about safe things and establish my credentials early, and walk a narrow path so I don't make any mistakes and don't do anything too risky and offend them, or make them not like me."

You can see how exciting that talk is going to be. Ho hum. Wake me when it's over.

It was impossible for me to succeed from that position. There was no freedom in it. There was no strength or love or joy or energy.

But once I could rehearse and create in my own heart and mind a self-concept of a loving energy that really connects (and in my rehearsal I could go back over where that's happened in the past), then I could re-anchor that and reconfirm it with *me*. Now I could say, "That's me. Universal love and creativity. That's the real me. That's who I am."

You can do concept-anchoring with *anything*. No matter what task lies before you. You see yourself being able to drive the mountain road safely and also get there on time. Now you can enjoy yourself on the ride. You actually picture that. That's a mind shift that shifts the world for you.

It's the biggest, most exciting change in human psychology in the past hundred years! And that is the fact that ordinary human beings can internally wake up to who they are. They don't need decades of therapy or meditative training to do that.

Because they have the ability to see that it's all made up anyway. And it's not a bad thing that it's all made up. It's a beautiful, powerful, creative thing. When you see that your brain is there to create reality for you—and that's *why* you have a brain—everything becomes a creation. Instead of an externally-produced crisis.

The kingdom of heaven is within you.

The Wizard of Oz says look inside yourself and find self. God says look inside yourself and find the Holy Spirit. The first will get you to Kansas. The latter will get you to heaven. Take your pick.

~ **Max Lucado**

62

Helpless is the face of opportunity?

Tracy Goss in her book *The Last Word on Power* wrote:

> Death is not the most profound loss or tragedy in life. That which dies inside of us as we live is a far greater loss. The loss of possibility. A loss that comes from running our personal rackets, has ravaged the lives of too many individuals who could have otherwise transformed the world.

So these rackets that we run are really belief systems built on a house of cards (of lies we tell ourselves). These are lies about how weak we really are and how helpless we are in the face of life's opportunities.

Ponder that irony! People become helpless in the face in opportunity!

Opportunity threatens them!

Because rather than grabbing the opportunity and creating something wonderful, they react negatively. They react with caution. They try to be safe. They fear making a mistake. They become paralyzed "trying to decide" what to do with the opportunity.

At any given moment, with any given opportunity, I am either creating or I am reacting.

If I'm creating, I'm coming from my highest self. I'm coming from the infinite creativity of the universe that is my very essence.

Our common mythology teaches us that *it's just so rare* that we really create. It's some kind of "epiphany!" when it happens. Like writers who believe they have to wait for inspiration to write. And they haven't been inspired for years. Some writers go into depression and get what they believe is "writer's block." Writer's block is just a concept, but they can't see it. They think it's a real block.

A creative life is simpler than that.

Begin by thinking in terms of creating rather than reacting. See the choice that's always present. If you catch yourself reacting, all that means is that you are low on your ladder. You're stuck in your left brain. You're trapped in there and you're condemning things. Condemning and judging is how you know you're there!

Notice how opportunity arrives and rather than welcome it, you start to judge it! You might spend your whole day looking that gift horse in the mouth.

Let the shift happen. Right then and there. See whatever is in front of you as an opportunity, and then use it to begin creating what you want.

All my life I've looked at words
as though I were seeing them
for the first time.

~ **Ernest Hemingway**

63

A soothing rainbow of relaxation

Language is the house of Being. In its home we dwell.
Those who think and those who create with words
are the guardians of this home.

~ Martin Heidegger

Language is the house of being! And this house of being is built with words. So it should not be so surprising to see the lasting effect that these "mere" words have.

You can test this effect any way you like. But do test it. Test it with yourself. Start with three words that are positive for you. Let's say, "soothing," "rainbow," "relaxation." Those are three words that are usually positive for people.

So now say to yourself, "soothing, rainbow, relaxation" and notice the feeling in your body when you say it. Say it again out loud. And again. Notice how you feel as you ponder these three words. Notice that there's really a change in how you feel. You start to breathe a little more easily and deeply, you're a little more relaxed, and all of a sudden life looks a little more attractive to you.

And it was all from pondering the words soothing, rainbow, and relaxation. Those three words (as you reflect on them) will alter the chemistry in your body, will completely change the biomarkers, as they can be measured, and will shift your brain waves.

Now think of the words, "fatal," "pornographic," "life-threatening." Those three words usually put people on edge. If you were to keep saying them to yourself you would become edgy. Soon you'd be deeply upset.

Just words, though, right?

You can also test this by sending an email to someone. Send somebody you know an email that says "soothing, rainbow, relaxation" and then sign your name, and see what kind of reactions you get. Send it to 20 people and then send the email that says, "fatal, pornographic, life-threatening" and sign your name and see what kind of reactions you get to that! These are just words. But look at the emotions they trigger in people!

Always, all day, night and day—even when you are asleep—certain words and phrases pass through the mind. When you are in the dream level of consciousness (at the Alpha brainwave state) words are still seeding their impact. Certain words and phrases that went into your mind during the day can manifest at night in a really bad dream. Because the brain at night tries to resolve the unfinished business of the day, and it will try to complete those word pictures for you. Really bad dreams and nightmares occur because certain thoughts keep coming in that you haven't seen for what they are. At night the dream tries to complete the unfinished thoughts of the day. It can be frightening.

But they're words—that's all they are.

Let's just pick one word for now and see its impact. The word will be "problem."

Most of us have a very negative emotional history with the word problem. If someone calls you and says, "We've got a problem," notice how you feel. It's not good. If you grab it and cling to it, it can take you down the ladder.

The very use of the word "problem" diminishes your problem-solving ability. What a double-bind that is. By identifying and naming a "problem" I've lowered my ability to solve it. No wonder I have so many problems piling up!

The very use of the *word* shrinks the resources I once had to solve things. That was the last thing I wanted when I brought this problem up. I thought I had courageously spoken about this problem in order to see it and solve it. Yet now I've created my own weakness. Because the mere mention of the word has lowered my mood, and therefore lowered my consciousness and creativity, the very things I need to solve things with.

What a load of quicksand that is. The mind has undercut itself with language! When it does this, language is truly the house of being.

So it's time to allow an immediate mind shift. Because if I open my mind, it will shift my perception of the world around me and its "problems." So now I'll try describing this situation (the one I was tempted to call a problem) as "a real adventure." I might now identify it as a real *opportunity*. And the more I use this new language, the faster my mind opens and rises.

Try sending ten people an email with just the word "problem" in it then sign your name. See what they come back with. Watch all the nervous responses! "Hey, what's going on? Call me! What problem? What do you mean? What are you referring to? Do you mean that voice mail I left? I'm sorry, I might have been too harsh!"

It will trigger all kinds of negative response. But it's just a word. Now, find 10 different people and send them a one-word email that says "opportunity." And sign your name. Watch what happens to *that* email. "Hey, great to hear from you! Wow, I want to talk about that opportunity whatever it is. Opportunity for me and you? Call me!"

You have a completely different response. Because you shifted the language.

Life's splendor forever lies in wait around each one of us in all its fullness, but veiled from view, deep down, invisible, far off. It is there, though, not hostile, not reluctant, not deaf. If you summon it by the right word, by its right name, it will come.

~ Franz Kafka
The Diaries of Franz Kafka

64

You either own it or you don't

I'm often asked to give a public speech or a workshop on my book *Reinventing Yourself*, which contains the owner/victim distinction.

My workshops are always about contrasting distinctions. The workshops are never just downloads of information. People already have too much information.

Clients who are considering whether to hire me have asked, "What's the information in your speech?"

"There isn't much."

"Are you joking?"

"No. There's just a distinction."

"You'll have to explain that."

A distinction is different than information. If I went in front of a group of people for an hour and gave them a ton of new information, they'd simply have more information. Now they'd have to try to remember it all! They might have taken notes, but a month later they would have forgotten most of the information. Sounds like a waste of time. No wonder most leaders tell me, "Training comes and goes and nothing's ever different."

I agree with that. How could anything be different when you're just filling people with information?

These days we already receive more information than ever

before in the history of humankind. We are overwhelmed with information. We get so much. The minute we wake up, the television might be on, or the radio, or we flip the computer on to get our early morning information, or receive a series of texts, and soon the information just overwhelms us. It's like a rush of polluted water . . . a tsunami of information.

And then throughout the day we are given more and more information.

So if you go into a seminar and I give you even more information, then it's a disservice!

A single contrasting distinction is different than information. Because a distinction is simply a vision of separation. Over here is this, over there is that. The intention is to inspire an insight. And when you get a new insight, it never leaves you with anything you have to "try to remember."

Like the distinction between perceiving the world like an owner and perceiving it like a victim. A clear distinction. An unforgettable contrast. When you see it and when you "get" the contrast—it is yours forever.

You own your insight. You're like the young King Arthur of legend pulling the sword Excalibur from the stone. (Now the sword was his, and he would be the once and future king.)

When you clearly *get* how distinct two things are you'll never lose that distinction.

For example, life and death. It's a contrasting distinction! I believe you've already gotten that one. Because when you were a young child there was a point at which you learned about death, and how it was different and distinct from life.

I remember when I was three years old and there was a dead bird on the road. My father was pushing me in a stroller and I pointed at the bird and he explained to me that that bird was dead. And for the first time, I got the distinction. Something could be living or something could be dead.

Once you get a distinction, you've got it. You don't have to revisit it and continuously remind yourself of it.

I have had people contact me who were in an owner/victim distinction seminar over ten years ago and tell me that the main distinction has stayed with them throughout all these years.

When the sun goes down, it is night time. We know that because we learned the distinction between night and day. We only had to get it once. We never had to put a sticker up on our refrigerator saying, "Remember: dark equals night time and light equals day time." We never have to *remind ourselves* of a distinction. We've already got it.

Distinctions are like good jokes. You get it! When you get it, you own it. It's yours. You are now moving through the world interacting with others *with a distinction in you* that you have and can use. Distinctions help you simplify life. You have new mental leverage that wasn't there before. Shifting becomes easier.

Very little is needed
to make a happy life;
it is all within yourself,
in your way of thinking.

~ **Marcus Aurelius**

65

Victim thinking drags me down

A victim is someone who wakes up in the morning and interprets natural, normal events as threats and injustices. He then talks all day in victimized language, which deepens the problem. Language is the house of being for a victim, and it is a bleak house.

It's a self-fulfilling prophecy to think I'm a victim. Because when I speak victim language it carries me down to the lowest levels of productivity and creativity. And at those low levels I am less capable of solving problems or creating wealth or even creating relationships. All the things I wish I could do!

So now I become even *more* of a victim. My victim self-concept creates more victim language! Soon other victims gather around me to reinforce me. They tell me they are victims, too, and that it's real. They say it has nothing to do with the mind. It's just out there.

Meanwhile victim language causes low energy. So the problems are now piling up. Who has the energy to solve them? Who has the willpower? Who has the heart anymore?

Predators and manipulators see my vulnerable and weak state. Now I'm taken advantage of! And it's real stuff and true! Not in the mind at all! Now other people use me for things, and I never really get respect.

A victim talks about people who made her feel inferior.

Later in the day she singles out people who made her feel stressed. That's the victim's life. Her emotions are all caused by other people. Or so it seems.

No wonder she's now mildly afraid of other people. Can you blame her? Look how everyone makes her feel.

If I say to her, "Have a really great day," she might say to me, "Well I sure *hope* so, but how would I know if I was going to have a great day? How in the world would I know ahead of time whether today is going to be great?"

Whereas owners can actually say, "I will appreciate this day as a great day," and that's a primary difference between the two people. (Sometimes known as a distinction.)

When I'm a victim, I'll start my day by reviewing what I dread. I have dread for breakfast! What do I hope doesn't happen to me? What should I watch out for today?

"Oh, no, I have this darn meeting."

"Oh, my goodness, there's so much more to do today than I have time to do, what will I do?"

I'm already stressed just thinking about my day. And this thought-produced, stressed-out state makes me less effective. So I make mistakes. I forget to call someone back. I lock my keys in the car! My judgment is bad. I waste time needlessly. I avoid what's important.

Ownership is the opposite of that downward spiral. Its starting point is gratitude and awareness of my essential creativity. So rather than a desired state to *get to*, creativity is the beginning place—a place to come from.

A lot of times when people attend the owner/victim seminar, they'll come up to me later and say, "Now I've really got to be more of an owner. I heard what you said. I can see where that would really help my life and I know it's going to take a lot of work for me to do it. But I just know I'm going to be able to get there. Someday. If I read your book again and really practice?"

My answer is it's not a place to get to.

It's a place to come from. In fact, it's very natural. You're already there. Only thought can change that. Circumstances can't.

In the seminar I like keeping it as simple and distinct as possible. I have two flipcharts. That's it. No PowerPoint or multi-media overheads. I don't come into the course descending from the ceiling like David Bowie in *Ziggy Stardust and the Spiders from Mars*. The loud speakers aren't singing "Ground Control to Major Tom" when I walk in.

Some "motivators" like those approaches, but I'm not there to motivate anyone.

I'm there to uncover a gentle distinction.

One of the flipcharts I label "owner," the other I label "victim." I begin to put words on each flipchart. I write simple phrases. People sit and watch and look at the two different flipcharts as I walk back and forth between them. They can see victim thoughts. They let them sink in. They sit back and look at them in a very objective way. And then they can look at ownership thoughts (the language of owners of the human spirit, people who don't offer their spirit to others to be broken during the day).

I might quote Eleanor Roosevelt to further the distinction of owner. She said "No one can make me feel inferior without my permission."

I can see people reflecting on that remark. I actually see some of them realizing that no one can make them feel inferior without their permission.

The mind shifts.

I believe God wants you to know…
that all the problems you face today
are going to go away,
unless you worry them to stay.

~ **Neale Donald Walsch**

66

Why don't you know how to do it?

It's very interesting to me that people believe that what's missing in their lives is a knowledge of *how to* do something.

"I don't know how to get business," or "I don't know how to start," or "I don't know how to attract clients to me," or "I don't know how to let people know I'm available for work."

Well, the *how to* is never really what's missing here. In all my years of coaching people, when they have told me "I don't know how to," what's really true is: *I don't want to yet.*

I sometimes even tell them. Right out loud. Right after they have told me they don't know how to do something important.

"You just don't want to yet."

One man—call him Dodger (although that's not his real name)—I was working with had a wonderful business, tremendously beautiful service he offered, and a great number of clients who loved his work. But the business wasn't running at a profit. So he would say to me, "I don't know how to run a business. I don't know how to do this. This is the part I don't know how to do."

And it was funny, because I knew when he was saying this, that what he really meant was "I don't *want* to run a business. I've never *wanted* to know how to run a business. I've never really *wanted* to take full responsibility for running a business at a profit."

When your *want to* (that thing we'll call the "want to"—the desire) is strong enough, the *how to* comes quite quickly. You'll find it so fast it will be just amazing to you—when your "want to" is strong enough.

I have people come up to me and say, "I want to be a public speaker, but I don't know how to do it. How do you start? I don't know how to start."

I'm thinking to myself, "You don't want to be one yet," because if you wanted to be one, you would have found out how. You'd be in that library. On the internet. You'd be reading. It's all there.

Or you'd skip all that and you'd be speaking. Here, there and everywhere.

I remember when I finally had a burning desire to be a public speaker. I knew it was what I wanted to be able to do—to make my primary income from talking to groups. When I got full clarity and inner guidance I then knew I wouldn't stop at anything until I made that happen.

Once my desire (my "want to") was at that certain critical level, I became a tireless explorer. I was hunting down the "how to."

I was reading a book at the time (and I remember reading avidly, voraciously) by Napoleon Hill. And inside it he said he himself wanted to be a public speaker and didn't know how to start, so he decided to give some free talks. He had a friend who had a restaurant that was struggling and he said he would help the restaurant by giving free talks to attract people in there to hear him. The friend said yes. He had nothing to lose. So Napoleon Hill would come to this little restaurant once a week and talk. People started coming in because of his free talks. Soon he had a following and it got bigger and bigger and the restaurant started to thrive. The talk was free. Everybody won.

I got excited reading that! So I asked the president of a company I was working for if I could use our building to do a weekly free talk for people. He had a huge meeting room there, and it wasn't being used in the evenings. What if I gave a free talk every Tuesday night? Could I use the meeting room, and could I bring people in here?

He was skeptical, but indulgent. He said, "Well, sure, why not?"

So I began to pass out flyers at all the surrounding businesses to let people know—Tuesday night—goal achievement meeting! Bring your goals! We'll talk about how to achieve them. Free—it won't cost you anything.

The first Tuesday night meeting, two people showed up. There I was in front of the huge room and there are two people. But I decided to give those two people the best evening they ever had. I passed out little sheets that I made with lots of quotes on them about achieving goals, and blank areas for the exercises we would do. I was a single father with no babysitter so my kids sat in the class, too.

Six months later, the place was packed. It was overrun with people. The word got out, and I got better, and now some of the people attending started asking, "What do you charge to come into a company to do this?"

I also had begun to give free talks at places like Rotary, where other people came up and asked, "What would you charge to come talk to my sales team?" My career was getting launched. I didn't need to know *how to* become a public speaker because I was in action already doing it.

My way wasn't *the* way to do it—there are many other ways to do it—there are probably about a thousand different ways to do it. But finding a good "way" to do it is not the issue here. Because once I really *wanted* to, it was done. The power of commitment always handles that for you.

Anytime you want something to happen, and you find yourself telling yourself and other people that you don't know "how to" it is time for a mind shift.

Don't allow yourself to be pulled into that passive state of telling yourself you would love to do it, but you don't know how. That's never what's stopping you. What's true is *you don't want to yet*. And it doesn't really reflect badly on you that you don't want to yet. You can't want everything in life. You've got to choose, but only when you are ready. And you will know.

Simple can be harder than complex: You have to work hard to get your thinking clean to make it simple. But it's worth it in the end because once you get there, you can move mountains.

~ Steve Jobs

67

Doing what other people won't do

I was a garbage man. I had no problem with that job.
None. I'd go back and do it again if I had to.

~ Larry Bird

That's why Larry Bird became so great. He had no problem doing the work in front of him, no matter what that work was. He was willing to do the things other people didn't want to do.

Larry Bird's amazing career as a basketball star proved that it's not speed or genetics or athleticism that decides your success. It's doing the work that other people won't do. It's putting in the practice hours while others party on the buzz their name produces.

I can learn from this. I can ask myself what work I can do right now that looks unappealing to others in my field. What are the things I can do that others don't want to do. Actually seek, SEEK! what others avoid! And then do it with passion and creativity.

I accept chaos. I am not sure whether it accepts me. I know some people are terrified of the bomb. But then some people are terrified to be seen carrying a *Modern Screen* magazine. Experience teaches us that silence terrifies people the most.

~ Bob Dylan

68

Silence terrifies people the most

Terrified of being seen carrying a *Modern Screen* magazine is a terror I can identify with. I used to carry all sorts of magazines and books that I thought would give me a clue to the rich and famous, believing, erroneously, that they had some modern secret to living. Or that fame meant something.

I thought I wanted to live larger, and attain worldwide approval. Won't these magazines give me a clue?

If there is a clue somewhere it's in that other fear that Dylan identifies. The fear of silence. One of the most profound shifts in my life was from the fear of silence to the love of silence and solitude.

Dylan's great songs were written when he was sitting all alone. In the stillness. That same stillness is there for you and me, and it is a quantum field of creativity once the mind shifts down to full relaxation.

Inside you there is an artist you don't know about. Say yes quickly, if you know, if you've known it from before the beginning of the universe.

~ **Rumi**

69

Bring your music to the dance

Bring your hidden artistic talent to whatever you do. Don't have your business be separate and isolated from that talent. Oliver Wendell Holmes observed that "Most men die with their music still in them." Women, too. (Although according to all the old "famous quotations" you read, they didn't have women back then.)

My friend Andrew played King Arthur in a recent performance of Camelot that was so good that Kathy and I went to see it twice. Andrew is a life coach, public speaker and top real estate consultant.

Here's the point. What does Andrew's singing and musical creativity have to do with success in the business world?

Just everything.

Meister Eckhart claimed that "Should God stop singing all of existence would cease."

Almost every struggling small business I have ever coached has been missing precisely that element. They were people trying to make money by getting real grim about it. No artistic approach, no music in their hearts. So they made even less money. Then they got even more serious. Now they were failing even faster. Because the exact part of their brains that would have innovated and created breakthroughs for their business was being repressed by fear.

The best ventures always have rhythm, beauty and harmony in them. All your best movements do. When you're stuck on serious, find the music in you and feel the mind shift occur.

The perfect man of old
looked after himself first
before looking to help others.

~ Chuang Tzu

70

Take care of yourself first

I was coaching someone today—call her Simone—and she had lost a lot of the luster and enthusiasm she'd had in a previous session. She finally admitted that she was fatigued and sleep-deprived . . . up with her child until four in the morning, nursing coughs.

I asked her to take care of herself, to get plenty of rest.

I told her that sleep heals. I was drawing on painful personal experience. And success, when it's enduring, is always mind-body-spirit, never just one of those three, but always all three. You'll only fly high when all three are tuned. I told Simone, "Take care of yourself first."

But for a lot of people this is not easy.

They love serving people but they can't see that they themselves are also part of the "people" category. Part of the team. A vital part of the ecosystem. And always the best place to start when living a life of creative service.

Like the announcement in the plane that tells you to secure your own oxygen mask first, before your children's. If you try to do your children's first, everyone's in trouble. Because you yourself could pass out before they get their masks on. So serving yourself first is not selfish. It actually leaves you in better shape for helping others.

I know what it's like to care for children. My children's

mother was taken away from them when they were very young. She was hospitalized and was never able to fully return to the family setting. So there I was with full custody of four little ones! What an adventure.

But I learned quickly that to take care of them, I'd have to take care of me. Later it really hit home for me. The greatest gift I can give my child is the example of my own life working.

When a child sees a life that's working, it's a gift to that child.

So many parents think they need to be noble martyrs sacrificing their health and well-being for their children. But the children never wanted that. They would rather you be happy as a person. Do they really want a bitter, depressed, self-sacrificing parent who is giving all their time to *them*?

Delmore Schwartz wrote a short story called "In Dreams Begin Responsibilities." I choose to see those responsibilities as opportunities to *respond* compassionately to the people I love. To life. To opportunity disguised as trouble. And the more I rest and dream, the more enjoyable those responsibilities become. Rather than burdens, they are now gifts.

Don't waste life in doubts and fears; spend yourself on the work before you, well assured that the right performance of this hour's duties will be the best preparation for the hours and ages that will follow it.

~ Ralph Waldo Emerson
"Compensation"

71

No more newspapers to read?

Newspapers everywhere are going out of business, and many people are alarmed and worried. Some are even saddened.

But I always remember what Maria said in *The Sound of Music*—"When the good Lord closes a door, he always opens a window." It's reckless and foolhardy to ignore the wisdom of Maria Von Trapp, wouldn't you agree?

That same wisdom was the whole point of Emerson's profound essay, "Compensation." Everything is always compensated for. You can't lose something without gaining something else.

And, as Byron Katie says, "Loss is a concept." It's always and only just a concept.

So here I am loving and enjoying cable TV's many choices, all the great things on Netflix, and my favorite websites and blogs and news sources on the internet—far, far better than any newspaper is today, and yet I can still remain unaware of the divine law of compensation, always at work in the universe. I can still make myself sad. Over anything. With my thoughts. (If I don't focus on and cling to those thoughts of sadness in there, the sadness simply can't happen.)

The media feeds this sense of sadness. Today a TV show like *Meet the Press* should really be called something else . . . it should be called WHY YOU SHOULD BE DEPRESSED.

Some people view all change with deep alarm. Oh, no! Just when they thought they had it all figured out, major changes sweep through the world. And, oh no! (I used to watch my favorite duo Bud & Travis perform and in between songs while they were tuning their guitars Bud said, "When I get this guitar tuned I'm going to weld it.")

The sun comes up. The paper is inside now. I look through it. It only takes me seven minutes to read everything of interest. Most of what's in the paper I knew about yesterday or the day before—because of the internet.

So I set it aside and open the book I'm reading (for the third time) by Brenda Ueland called *If You Want to Write*. In it she says (and I see I have highlighted it in yellow) William Blake has inspired her on this subject of being creative. Blake said, "Imagination is the Divine Body in every person."

Brenda Ueland then says, "Blake thought that this creative power should be kept alive in all people for all of their lives. And so do I. Why? Because it is life itself. It is the spirit. In fact it is the only important thing about us. The rest of us is legs and stomach, materialistic cravings and fears."

She was a brilliant woman. Her book was written in 1938! Yet when I read it she is sitting right here in my kitchen with me. I can listen and really hear what she says—life is for creation—or I can turn on the news and be a *reactor* in life. That's the choice I always have.

When we're at our yellow-highlighting best we are creating the future together. The paradox of creating a great future is that it always takes place in the present moment: this little communication right here in front of me will have more to do with my future than any series of worries I may string together.

That next task you do, whatever it is, will have more to do with creating your future than any fearful, worried brainstorm of projection ever will.

Don't fight forces, use them.

~ Buckminster Fuller

72

Eventually you must serve someone

People today spend hours doing their social networking, getting connected and linked. I had a friend I'll call Charlotte who spent a full year linking people to her network, up to twelve hours a day at her computer weaving her virtual web, and at the end had to declare bankruptcy and move out of her foreclosed-upon home.

She never figured out why such successful computerized hooking-up never made her successful.

"Who is being served?" I would ask her about her "business."

"Tell me what you mean by that," Charlotte said.

"How are the people whose names you are now linked to being served?"

Silence.

Laurence Platt is a contemporary philosopher whose fascinating website is full of essays:

http://www.laurenceplatt.com/wernererhard/

Platt recently wrote this: "There are occasions of absolute greatness which come on the world from time to time, carefully orchestrated events which seem so simple, so effortless in their execution, so *natural* that they appear to be deceptively *easy*.

Almost always predicating such events is herculean preparation, heroic, inspired *bringing forth*, driven setups, corrections, testing, then more corrections, still *more* testing and still more corrections before the final product is ready for the world."

This process that Platt is describing is so much more powerful and committed than hooking up and giving shout-outs. I am stunned by how beautifully he finishes his observation:

"When the finished product finally appears, it's hailed as masterful, as *genius*, as a *champion of the genre*. We know something happened prior to this to get it into the shape it's in. But we almost aren't ever privy to exactly what it takes. *We weren't there* to see what it takes to bring it forth in the state of mastery."

To shift in the mind from mere social networking to really and truly working on something great that *profoundly serves people* is to shift from living on the shallow surface of life to diving toward the treasures of the deep.

People living deeply
have no fear of death.

~ **Anaïs Nin**

73

Absolutely top heavy with expectations

Now let's revisit the earlier point I made about the weakness of expectations versus the creative power of agreements. Let's take a look at a hands-on practical application.

I was hired to coach and train a major international company in Ohio recently because they had all kinds of performance and productivity breakdowns. I was asked to go train their people using the owner/victim distinction. (Owners are aware that feelings come from thoughts on the inside and victims cling to the belief that feelings come from outside sources of causation: other people and circumstances and situations.)

The hope was that morale might be lifted among the people on the assembly line who were creating the products once they found a better understanding of where their resentment was coming from. And the hope was that after the training, better efficiency might follow.

Well, the real problem wasn't on the line, although morale was low and efficiency was poor. The real problem (as always) was in the leadership. (A fish rots from the head down.)

The leaders had nothing but expectations. They expected a lot from their people. They would walk around all day expecting things—they expected levels of job performance, they expected quotas to be met, expected quality standards to be hit, and expected customer deadlines to be met! They expected their directives to be followed and their emails to be eagerly read. After all, their subordinates were grown-ups with good jobs! They ought to behave accordingly. Why should I be a babysitter?

Their heads and hearts were heavy with expectation and the inevitable disappointment and despair that is built in to a life of expectation.

And then there were the stressed-out people on the manufacturing line. They were *trying* to live up to the expectations of the leaders, but really resenting the leaders in the process. Some of them told me that most of the expectations were unreasonable, and that the leaders didn't really understand how understaffed they were and how stressed they had become.

So, the whole place was in a morale crisis.

As I moved among the leaders, and talked to them, trying to figure out "how we can fix this," they told me about a certain employee who wasn't living up to expectations.

I said, "So what is that expectation?" and they would say, "Well, we expect him to get this job done by Friday so the customer can have the delivery on Monday. The customer expects it. We promised the customer the job on Monday, so we want it finished at the plant by Friday."

"Ok, great. So what happened?"

"Well, it wasn't done, and it wasn't done until the next Thursday, so the customer was very upset . . . and this has happened so often that we have lost our preferred status with the customer and everything has gone downhill."

"Well," I said very quietly, "Who was in charge of that product being done?"

"The line supervisor in the plant!"

Then I asked him a question that startled him (or at least quietly seemed to leave him without a way to respond).

I said, "What was your agreement with him?"

And he looked at me as if I had asked him, "Have you taken a ballet lesson lately?" or some other very strange question, and he didn't answer. So I asked him again what the agreement was with his employee on the finishing of that job.

Then he said, "What do you mean by that?"

I said, "On the matter of getting this done by Friday, what was your agreement?"

"You mean I have to have an agreement with everybody?"

"Let's just look at that one job in question."

"Are you saying I've got to go around and get an agreement for every job? He *knew* I expected it by Friday, he got my e-mail, he knew the customer was expecting it by Monday. I don't want to have to go hold his hand. He's a professional, I'm a professional . . . "

"But expectations don't seem to be working. Or am I missing something? Expectations aren't being met."

"Well I don't know why that is!"

We had a long talk about expectations. I asked him how he felt when other people expected something of him, versus how he felt when they had taken time to create an agreement with him. He began to acknowledge that expectations might be counter-productive.

He finally got an insight: People do not enjoy trying to live up to expectations. In fact, people usually rebel against expectations. Employees don't like it that you simply expect things of them without involving them in the process. There's no respect in that.

And so we decided to experiment with leading-by-agreement instead of leading-by-expectation. We invited the line supervisor in and we all sat down. After discussing an upcoming job the leader said, "Can you agree to have this job ready by Friday?"

And the line supervisor said, "Well, I would like to . . . but I'm a little under-staffed so I can't promise it for sure."

And the leader looked a little startled and said, "What can you promise for sure?"

"If you gave me one extra person to work on it, I could promise it Friday, for sure. If I don't have an extra person, I can promise it next Tuesday for sure."

The leader thought for a while and he said, "I'll give you an extra person. Right away. I'll talk to HR as soon as we're finished. Now, with an extra person what can I count on?"

"Well, you can count on Friday."

"Thank you," and they shook hands.

That's an agreement. That's so much *stronger* than an expectation, and it also leads to effective, timely completion of work, because of the binding spirit of collaboration. It just flat out works, even though leaders often think, when they ponder the concept, that it would lead to an unnecessary, time-wasting agreement meeting. But when they go beyond the concept, and are willing to explore and experiment with it, they find that it saves time.

Most new people I work with who are leaders don't realize the power of agreement. They don't understand that their leadership anxiety comes from the expectations they are carrying around all day.

When I first talk to them I ask what's going on.

"Well, I've got problems with this person, I've got problems with that person," and I find out the reason they have problems is because they don't have agreements. They have expectations and the expectations are not being met.

Once they shift their minds up to the art form known as creating agreements, they start feeling more like partners with their people and morale immediately improves. Sometimes it takes courage to try this out, but I've never seen creative collaboration fail as a leadership process, especially in comparison to leading-by-expectation and micromanagement.

There is a mind-shifting principle behind this story. It might look like it's merely a business management technique that only applies to organizations. But when I look more mindfully at what's occurring, I can see it applying to all relationships everywhere.

A co-created agreement is like a co-written song. It has beauty and artistic satisfaction in it.

"My husband never picks up his socks. It drives me crazy. It's so disrespectful. It feels so demeaning to me to have to pick up after him like I'm some servant."

Do you talk to him about it?

"Oh I've complained a lot. I've lost my temper over it, so yes. One night I left the house for two days and stayed with my mother.

"Then I felt bad and came home. When I got there you know what I found? Socks on the floor of the bathroom! I blew up."

You can see where that situation is headed. And it isn't a happy place. But when the woman with the sock-expectation was able to open her mind we talked about the possibility of creating an agreement. It took a few tries but the two of them found a time when they were both in good moods and they created an agreement around the socks. To this day it has been kept.

I'm not in this world to live up to your expectations and you're not in this world to live up to mine.

~ Bruce Lee

74

Well, what do you expect?

If you are a person who walks around with expectations of other people, only two things can happen and neither of them is good.

1) People don't live up to your expectation! Well, that's not fun. You're disappointed. Sometimes you're even feeling betrayed if it was a serious expectation.

2) The other thing that can happen is that they do live up to it! Now what? Well, you're just neutral—nothing—you *expected* it. So you say "Daisy showed up to the meeting on time," you think, "but that's what I expected, so what?"

So, you either have "so what?" which is a life of boring nothingness, or you have disappointment. Those are your two experiences of other people.

We all know people whose main conversational theme is their disappointment in others. If they were in the movie *Dances with Wolves* their Indian name would be Disappointed In Others.

"I'm so disappointed in my son, I'm so disappointed in my managing partner, I'm so disappointed in my spouse. I feel betrayed by my ex-spouse—totally betrayed."

That's life in a world of expectations. Riding high in April, shot down in May.

But expectations are not necessary. You can live without them quite happily. You have agreements or you don't. And that becomes total freedom. Talk about a mind shift! It's actually possible to have no expectations of anyone (ahhh, I can just relax), and only have agreements when you want them.

* * *

What an unexpected pleasure life is to a child. Have you ever watched a child running around discovering things? That's how we were meant to live, we think as we watch them.

What happens to us as we grow older? Why do we lose that ongoing sense of unexpected pleasure?

I believe it is because our expectations start to accumulate, and weigh us down. When we accumulate enough of them life becomes almost unbearable.

A lot of times my work involves coaching clients who are having problems with their partner—their spouse—their life partner—whatever is the politically correct way to say it these days.

They're having trouble with "love."

They might have had a fight with their partner and so today in the coaching session at their office they're gloomy. I sit down and we're talking about productivity, performance and profit, but they're not having fun with this, so I finally say, "What's going on?" and they say, "Well, I had a fight with my wife and I'm kind of depressed today."

Now it's really important to see that *expectation versus agreement* is an even more useful mind shift in personal relationships than it is at work.

In personal relationships, the more expectations I have the more anxious, fearful and depressed I will be with my family.

Because my family members are just innocently going

around being human. So they can't be causing all this pain. It must be something else. And it is. It's expectation.

Because if I have no expectations, I really can't be upset. If I don't expect my dog to make me dinner I'm never upset when he doesn't.

Is it possible to have no expectations of the people you care most about? I've worked with people who have learned to do it. To go home, and walk into their house, and be carrying absolutely no expectations whatsoever of any person in that home.

When you have no expectations, the only thing that's possible is fresh adventure. Continuous surprise. If your loved one does something nice for you, what a nice surprise. If he says something nice, and you didn't expect anything, you are living in pure delight.

If he says something negative or edgy, it doesn't floor you, because you didn't expect anything. It's easier to get to neutral if you start in neutral. You're already there. Most people spend most of their emotional lives fighting to get from upset to neutral so they can have a civil discussion. It's much easier to be accepting of others if that's where you begin.

When you don't expect anything to begin with you can flow with whatever is said. And whenever you want to, you can let the words roll off of you like water off a duck.

Soon your loved ones are realizing that you are not continuously disappointed in them. What freedom that gives them to relate to you in more open and positive ways. How easy to create an agreement from that position!

A lot of people think, "If I have negative feelings, if I'm judging someone critically, if I'm upset with someone, it's *healthy* to just say it. It's *healthy* to judge and attack sometimes, it's *healthy* even to hurt someone else, because that takes the hurt out of me; and if I say something hurtful to you it's because the hurt in me needs to find another place to go!"

But how sensible and loving is that, really?

I had a client who said he had a fight with his wife and I asked him "How was it?" and he said, "Well, *you know*, you've had those."

And I said, "No, I really haven't."

"Oh, come on," he said.

I said, "I really haven't. Kathy and I have been together for over twenty-five years, and we've never had what people would call a fight."

He said, "Well . . . I . . . oh . . . yeah . . . okay . . . I forgot you're a saint, right? But I'm not, I'm a regular person."

"No, no, it's not that, I'm not a saint at all. In fact if you look at my biography I probably shouldn't be allowed to walk the earth a free man. So I'm not a saint, but I'll tell you that I don't fight with her and it's for the same reason that I don't punch the pizza delivery boy when he's late, or I don't strangle a cat in my backyard and kill it. Same reason exactly. I don't want to. I've decided that is not the kind of thing I want to do. So I won't do it. It's not useful."

Some people say that fights are great. They clear the air, they purge things, they're so wonderful. They make life worth living!

But the only people I've ever heard say that are now divorced. Because, no, fights are not wonderful. They're hurtful. They can be unforgettably hurtful, and they're mean and they're selfish. It's like two children just scratching each other's eyes out. Two tantrums indulged together.

You can lose your vision that way.

So, even in personal relationships, expectations are toxic and they serve no purpose. If they served a purpose, I'd be open to having them. But it's depressing to walk around with a ton of expectations for other human beings.

If I'm a true leader, and you're consistently late for my team meeting . . . that's on *me*. That's my lack of leadership. I have not taken the time to create a strong agreement with you. Then I'm too much of an ignoramus to see that I can take positive and constructive responsibility for the fact that I have a team that thinks it's okay to stroll in late to meetings. I'm too much of a victim thinker; I make that all about *you* and I even say to you the "e" word! "I expect you to be on time!"

What happens when I use the "e" word? When most people hear the word "expectation" they go down their ladder into a very rebellious, nasty state. Whenever they hear the word. Try it out. When people start telling you what they expect of you, feel how you feel it in the pit of your stomach. Feel how you tense up and get defensive right away. It doesn't bring people closer, it drives them apart.

Let's say you show up late for the meeting and I call you aside later (I don't want to embarrass you in front of the whole room) and I say, "I expect you to be on time for our meetings."

Whenever you hear what some other (superior!) human being expects of you, notice the feeling in your body. Is it warm? Does it open you? Do you feel like embracing that person? No. What usually happens when you hear the "e" word—expectation—is you get a knot in your stomach, you clench up, you get tight, you contract, and you start building your defense. You begin to defend against what the other person expects.

Human beings know, intuitively and deep down, that they were *not* put on this planet to live up to the expectations of others.

Therefore, whenever you use the expectation word, you inspire subtle rebellion, and now there's *less* likelihood that what you expect will happen. *Less* likelihood by expecting it!

So by expecting something to happen, you make it *not* happen.

I've never seen expectations work. I've never witnessed any kind of positive benefit they have in any relationship (personal or otherwise). I've never seen expectations bring people closer together. I've never seen an expectation make one partner more faithful.

I've never seen it do anything but alienate. Every time it is used inside the human system.

What I *have* seen work, beautifully, on the other hand, is *agreements*.

Human beings do not like breaking their word. And I mean all human beings including criminals. You know the loyalty oath, you know that honor among thieves is more than a concept. It's very real. It wasn't just made up by novelists and screenwriters. People will want to keep their word.

For the last ten years I've worked with leaders who move away from leading people through expectations and move over to agreements. They are very surprised. They have told me, "I don't think he'll keep the agreement." And they were pleasantly surprised.

And if he does break the agreement, and doesn't keep his own word, then that's a beautiful opportunity to have another, more basic discussion. To check whether that agreement was two-sided, a true agreement. That can be a very powerful conversation. When you give me your word, will you keep it? Can I count on it? Will you not give me your word if you don't intend to keep it? Can we start there?

Because if we don't have that fundamental agreement, how can we have a relationship? If someone will actually tell you that their word means nothing, that they are going to lie to you, they are going to tell you that they are going to do something and then not do it, you can't have that person even as an employee; because the basic social contract is not there. We count on our words meaning something!

People will keep their agreements such a high percentage of the time you don't need to worry about the few times they don't. And the times when they don't are such wonderful opportunities to sit down with them and say, "Let's look at our basic relationship with each other and how we can start over with a change of heart."

Do any of these futilities sound familiar?

"I expect *you* to make *me* feel romantic and attractive."

"I expect *you* to make *me* feel appreciated."

"I expect *you* to make *me* feel loved and celebrated for bringing money home."

"I expect *you* to make *me* feel how I want to feel."

If I walk into a conversation expecting something of the conversation, I can't be open to all possibilities anymore. I can't listen generously to the other person. I can't be surprised or surprising. I can't really have fun. I can't be compassionate and discover new things about you.

It's running into someone or something *unexpectedly* that is the most fun in life.

"What an unexpected pleasure!" people say when they see you on the street, giving the secret of happy relationships away right there.

But can we hear them when they say it—are we really listening? What . . . an . . . *unexpected* . . . pleasure.

There's no pleasure like it.

An unexpected pleasure.

Life can be filled with unexpected pleasures. When you allow this shift in your mind, you find this out again.

And the beauty of shifting away from expectations is that I shift away from being at the mercy and at the effect of everyone else. I now take full responsibility for my happiness, for my financial well-being, for my energy level. It's back to me. It's not on *you* anymore and the good thing about it being back to me, is that I'm the only one I can really work on anyway.

I am open to the guidance of synchronicity, and do not let expectations hinder my path.

~ **Dalai Lama**

75

To make more money, go non-linear

What is it that when I am doing it, time really is not an issue?

In other words, when I am doing that thing, I can look at the clock and say "Oh, my goodness, where did that hour go? I can't believe it's six o'clock!"

When I can't believe time has passed so quickly it's because I have left behind the linear world of measured time. You know that linear world. It goes tick-tock, tick-tock. That's its soundtrack. Time just creeping by to the beat of a boring drum.

I remember jobs, and classes I had to sit through, where I kept looking at the clock . . . and that clock looked like it was the slowest thing in the world. I couldn't wait for that time to be over.

I remember working in some factories where that clock would just go by so slowly. We would watch the clock, then we would try not to watch the clock. That was a good sign that we were not engaged in our best work. Nor did we have the shifting capacity to have that not matter. (Because with the right number of mind shifts, everything I do becomes my true calling.)

If you want to start something exciting on your own, you don't have to quit your job to do it. You can do a little bit of it here and there and let it grow nicely on the side. Once you get the signs that it's up and running and that it can support you, boom . . . you're gone and that's what you do.

Other friends of mine have left the company they are with, and then sold themselves back to that company as a consultant, so now they only go in one or two days a week, do their very best thing, get a nice fee for that, and use the other four days for things they love to do even more.

So in today's global market, with all the leverage that the internet gives you to reach out to the world instantly, it's much easier to find what you love to do and tap into it.

We have the ability to link love, service and wealth together! In the past those three things were rarely linked. That was not the key to making money. Today it is. If we're enlightened enough to see it, the global internet marketplace is fertile enough to receive it. It's a mind shift: Love, service, wealth. Love, service, wealth. If I can get that pattern going—get that rhythm—get that chanted mantra in my mind, I can succeed. What do I love to do for people? How can I serve more people with it? Wealth will come as a result of that.

In the past, it was different. In the very near past it was loyalty to an organization, duty, and obligation. You had to figure out a way to earn a living, then win a position, somewhere. It was all a STRUGGLE in which bootlicking and apple-polishing were indispensable tools for advancing. It was often about manipulating, office politics and winning people over. Playing the game of sucking up! All the old style, hierarchal structures of companies and governmental organizations are based on the old monarchical systems of the past. People mastering the licking of boots. People becoming more and more skillful at polishing apples for the teacher.

Those systems emphasized that there were superior humans and subservient humans. But that whole paradigm is being dissolved by powerful individuals who do what they love, then sell it, and make a lot of money, and keep the world turning. It's a positive mind shift that has shifted the world.

If you give it good concentration, good energy, good heart and good performance, the song will play you.

~ Levon Helm

76

How to have more energy

People I talk to are always looking for more energy. They have this long list of things they think they need to get done so they say, "Boy, I wish I had more energy. What can I do for more energy? What foods can I eat that give energy? What exercise can I do? I wish I had more energy for my day."

And they look in many different places for energy because they have so much to do.

One place they don't look but could, is here: purpose.

Purpose actually produces energy.

When I was a little boy I used to go swimming with friends and I remember a couple of times while playing around in the lake one of my friends would hold me under water. Just playing around. He would hold me down there under water for a while just to scare me. Just to have some fun and to make my heart race.

Well, I never had so much energy as when that happened. I was focused! I wasn't distracted by anything other than the fight to get up above water. That was it. I wasn't worried about when I would have to go to bed that night—I wasn't thinking about a thousand other things. I was simply focused on getting up above the water. Never in my life have I ever had so much energy.

I read a lot of accounts and I've seen some documentaries

and movies made about people who break out of prison—an impossible prison to break out of. Yet day and night they plan. Amazing things happen when people wake up with their purpose—a singular purpose. Throughout the day that purpose is with them so they see everything in the context of that purpose. Every little thing about the guards, the ventilation system, the courtyard, everything is potentially useful to the breakout.

Throughout the day they ask, *how could I use this*? What's useful in this? What's useful here based on what I'm up to?

We can all have such a purpose. It's just made up. And when we do make one up, we can now convert what for other people shows up as "bad news" into useful news. When other people get "bad news" they allow themselves to slide down their rungs and be in a bad mood. Loss of energy! Now they're in their least resourceful state: disheartened and discouraged and not feeling so great. That's what "bad news" seems to do to them when it's not seen clearly as a mere fleeting thought.

But, when you have allowed and experienced a shift in your mind and now you bounce back up to where you realize you are *up to something*, all of life is different. The expression on your face and the movement of your body is different. (We observe our little boy moving quickly through the living room to the porch, and we say, "He's up to *something*.")

When any news at all comes to you in this state, you simply ask, "Given what I am up to in life, how can I use this?"

When those prisoners wake up in the morning and they look around, everything they see and everyone they talk to filters through the ongoing inquiry, "How do I break out of this place?" and then, "How does this situation help me with the plan I've got going on to break out?" Because that's all they're thinking about—that's what they are focused on: breaking out—breaking free.

We can break free, too.

Being up to something in our professional business life

gives us energy and makes us enjoy that life. So I recommend it highly that the question (what am I up to?) is in your work day forever, so that you can really know the difference (in how it feels) to be living from purpose versus living from random anxieties about the future.

You can turn a conservative bank president into a garbage-eating bum just by killing off some of the brain cells that contain the bio-computer program for his personality. If you damage other areas of the brain, you can erase all memory.

~ **Christopher Calder**

77

You can focus or you can spray

Living from my anxieties is a completely different way of life. Unlike living from purpose, there is very little energy available.

And most of my anxieties come from trying to protect my personality, my ego, and my smallest sense of being a separate self. And because this separation is false, it is fraught with problems.

My egoic personality can be constantly wounded and disrespected. It's whole purpose is an everlasting fight for respect. A battle I can never win.

But living from purpose has other people's opinions of me not feel so important.

When I am up to something, energy flows *into* me. But when I am focused on the isolated and separate self that I think I am (my personality), energy flows *away* from me.

Personality fixation leaves me weakened because everyone and everything else looks so threatening and powerful. Other people look like they have all the money and all the power my personality needs. Institutions look overwhelmingly intimidating. Health problems, no matter how small, now look like they could take me down. Everything looks frightening when I'm living from my personality.

We read a lot of amazing stories about people who become

more and more successful with age. People like Clint Eastwood, or Frank Lloyd Wright or Helen Mirren, or Judi Dench or P.D. James, who really start to blossom in their 70's and 80's because they've stayed on their curve of artistic purpose . . . a curve that keeps eliminating what's not important.

I've always loved this quote by the great ballet director, George Balanchine. He says, "I've got more energy now than when I was younger because I know exactly what I want to do."

He has *more* energy now than when he was younger. And it's because he knows exactly what he wants to do.

When Balanchine was younger (like so many of us) he had so many things he was trying to do at once. Energy is robbed by this kind of indecision. Not choosing freely what to do next. Trying so hard to decide which course to take. It wears you out.

That's why I love the old saying, "Winners focus, losers spray." It's really true.

When my sense of purpose floods me with energy—single-minded energy—it's really a beautiful thing.

There's a story I love to tell about Harry Bernstein. People misinterpret the story sometimes to be about doing great things in your old age. It's not about that. It's about mind shifting from personality to purpose. Shift the mind, shift the world.

Harry was ninety-three years old. His wife had just died of leukemia and he was sad and he didn't know how to go on because his purpose prior to then was taking care of her, and being with her and making sure she was happy. So all of a sudden—at ninety-three years old—this man's purpose drops out from under him and he wakes up—and there's no more energy for living.

That's depression. He was depressed—what's the use—why bother—why go on—that's the whole concept of depression—*I'm up to nothing.* There's nothing I'm enthused about or excited about. So now the focus is back on lonely personality . . . me . . . my feelings . . . how I'm feeling about this and what I think about that and my sadness. My sadness, my remorse and my regret—a totally self-centered focus.

But Harry Bernstein didn't stay in that world for long. His body shifted from depression the moment his mind shifted from personality to purpose.

He did something unusual and we don't know quite what inspired him. When the mind shifts, spirit has a way in. Like Leonard Cohen sings, there is a crack in everything, that's how the light gets in. Harry Bernstein decided to do something illogical.

He sat down and decided he would write about his life. So many things had occurred in his life, so many fascinating things. He would no longer just react to the death of his wife and take it personally.

Instead, he would create.

He would create a book that other people could read that would be all about the excitement, the sadness, all the amazing things that can happen to a human being who is ninety-three years old and has lived such a full, interesting life. He decided to create his life one more time, and this time he was going to create it as a book that would give other people great pleasure.

He was ninety-three! He wasn't twenty-five years old and learning to be an author and making connections with posh people in the publishing world and getting on a social network and finding out who the good agents were, planting seeds for the future. How much of a future is there when you are ninety-three? Anybody?

Most people waste 90 percent of their days on the future. And maybe I'm just guessing at that. I can say however, that I used to waste 90 percent of my own days thinking about my thoughts about the future. I was always trying to find other people to connect to who would make me successful someday. It's just a sad scattering of intellectual power and imagination with the false idea that I have got to know someone else who is powerful who will pull me up into the lofty and exclusive ranks of power.

But what Harry Bernstein did is what anyone can do—what all of us can do—even if we're eighteen years old. We don't have to wait until we're ninety-three. We can create a purpose. We don't have to focus all day on the feelings we are feeling produced by thoughts about our personality—we can have a purpose, and the purpose will then drive us.

Harry spent a year working around the clock on that book and then Harry found a publisher (after all the New York publishers rejected his work) at the London office of Random House. (This was back when you had to have a publisher for your book to get out to the world.) His manuscript sat there for over a year and then it came across the desk of an editor by the name of Kate Elton who read his book and said it was "unputdownable" (that was her word). Unputdownable!

That's what happens when you are working from a central purpose. He woke up with his purpose and he lived with his purpose, just like the guys breaking out of prison, just like me fighting to reach the surface of the lake in the water—there was nothing but that purpose.

Some people worry that if they shift their mind from their worries to a purpose it would be dangerous. It might make them fanatical. It might rule out other people. It might bring on disappointment.

Not so. Purpose can be more gentle than that. It can rest easy on the soul. It can be a very sweet presence that you wake up with in the morning. You can bring it with you. It's a friend to you. It never has to leave you. It's not something that you *try to remember* what it is, or *try to find out* what it is—it's there with you now. Just let it guide you. Get your thoughts out of its way. Allow your thoughts to be irrelevant to what you are creating.

If heartaches were commercials,
we'd all be on TV.

~ John Prine

78

How to use whatever reality gives

When I live life based on my personality anxieties, my whole world can be about hurt feelings. I've been there.

My daughter hurt my feelings when she didn't call me on my birthday. You hurt my feelings when you didn't answer my email. I swing like a monkey from hurt to hurt because it's all about my fragile personality that I'm trying to hold together. This *thing* I think is "me" that can be hurt and can be bothered and disrespected—unappreciated.

When people live from this personality anxiety and not from their purpose, life is not creative and life is no longer fun.

When people live from a created purpose, everything simplifies. Soon they can be like Fats Domino singing that he's simply "walking to New Orleans." (I remember when I was a teenager listening to him rocking and rolling and singing "I'm walkin' to New Orleans" and I just thought about how *simple* his life had become! That's all he was doing—he was walking to New Orleans. That was it. That was how joy worked.)

The other side of that (the dark side, the flip side) is my complex personality. The thoughts and beliefs about little old "me" that drive me crazy. Soon my mission on this flip side is to change other people so they won't hurt my "me" so much.

But if I pay attention I can allow experience to show me that wanting other people to change how they relate to me is a non-starter. It's dead in the water.

Wanting *myself* to change is where the juice is. Learning my spiritual nature is how it happens.

Because maybe I'm up to something and maybe the way I'm behaving or the way I'm spending my precious imagination and mental energy is not taking me there. So what can I change in me? I'll sit down with myself. Or maybe I'll even sit down with a mentor, or my coach, and I'll say, "Here's what I'm up to, and here's where I'm stuck."

He says, "Are you willing to change and see something that you're not used to seeing?"

"Yes."

"See it until realizing it becomes second nature to you?"

"Yeah, sure, because I'm up to something big."

"OK, let's work on that".

So now I'll be open to seeing something.

Recently I saw on the sidelines of a pro football game one of the players screaming at his coach. He was just losing it. Yelling at his coach and the coach was telling him to "knock it off," and yelling back at him. Pure public tantrum.

"You hurt my *feelings* when you don't put me in! I'm being disrespected! How do I look on national television when I sit out two plays that are important to the team? How am I coming across allowing myself to be disrespected like that?"

There was another player on the same team who for almost the whole season wasn't put in the game at all. He *used* that situation for his higher purpose. He took what reality gave him and said to himself, "I will rest. I will save my strength. I will learn. I will train. I will work out. I will be so fresh and ready when they *do* put me in that my purpose will be fulfilled."

And so it was. In the playoffs, that player was stronger than ever.

It does no good to search frantically for peace, to seek anxiously after love, joy or freedom. If you want joy, be joyful. If you want peace, be peaceful.

~ Cheri Huber

79

Stop trying to believe in yourself

Werner Erhard used to say, "The truth believed is a lie."

I didn't understand that at first. This point that he made so simply was a tough one for me to convince myself of. Especially because I was trying so hard to "believe in myself."

But I finally saw it. If there's a truth, such as the truth that we are all a part of an interconnected and infinite flow of creative energy, and if all I'm doing is *trying to believe it*, it's no longer a truth for me.

"I'm trying to learn how to believe in myself so I can charge a fee for my time," said a client I will call Claudius.

"Why do you need to believe in yourself?" I asked.

"Shouldn't I? I have always thought that I had to, or at least that I ought to."

"Why did you believe that you had to believe that?"

"Because without that, how can I do anything with confidence?"

"What if you were playing a part," I said, "a role on stage where your character had to speak to another character with total confidence?"

"I'd rehearse until I got it down."

"There you go! You just discovered the way out of all this mental confusion. It's exactly what you said it was, REHEARSE UNTIL YOU GET IT DOWN. Notice it is not called *try* to *believe* in yourself."

"I don't think I do believe in myself."

"Why would that matter? Why are you adding all this unnecessary mind-tripping to your life? Your actions lose their purity and strength when you try to believe in them. Everything becomes obscured by the ego's gratuitous attempts at generating belief in itself."

Pure awareness is better than belief. Action is better than all this attempted thinking. After taking enough action, the whole "believing in yourself" issue won't even be an issue. Because your action, your dance with the universe reveals to you the infinite creative energy that was "you" all long. You won't have to try to believe in yourself because you'll already have the awareness that surpasses belief. Your experience will bypass your thought system. You can ultimately rely on that experience instead of trying to believe a belief.

We are afraid of truth, afraid of fortune, afraid of death, and afraid of each other.

~ Ralph Waldo Emerson
"Self-Reliance"

80

Come let me dance with fear

Anaïs Nin was a prolific writer known for making fascinating books out of her journals. One of the entries to her diaries said, "And the day came when the risk to remain tight in a bud was more painful than the risk it took to blossom."

I know what it is to remain tight in a bud. I did that for so many years in so many aspects of my life. My music, my writing, my speaking, my profession, my relationships, my education . . . all tight in a bud. My world was shrinking in proportion to my lack of courage, which was profound. If a lack can be profound.

Once, when I was in basic training in the army, we had to do this obstacle course. I was an okay athlete when I was younger, playing a lot of sports (tentatively, never really full out) so I was able to do almost all of those physical obstacles— except one. There was one that I was terrified of. It was way up in the sky! It looked like a rope ladder to the moon! I got dizzy and sick to my stomach even looking up at how high that monstrous wooden tower stretched. We were supposed to climb a rope ladder all the way up and then . . . oh no way! . . . slide down the other side of the tower on a pulley on a rope! I froze with fear. This would not happen. It would not be possible.

Soon our platoon was marching toward this next obstacle. What was I to do? I really had to think fast. Right next to us was another platoon marching to a different obstacle station, one that our platoon had already done. As they marched next to us I started marching closer to them until I was right next to their outer line of people. I had to think fast, so I forced a stumble, a half-fall to the ground, and as I spun and pivoted in the gravel I got up and back in line . . . in the other platoon's line! I kept marching along hoping no one would catch on, and they didn't! I was now a part of the other platoon—and as I went through their obstacle with them (an easy one, crawling under rope nets with your rifle) I kept an eye out on my own platoon—my real platoon! My friends! I saw them! They were going up, up, UP! that godawful tower! And then sliding down! Poor souls! How do they do it? And when I noticed that they were finished and were marching off to their final obstacle, another easy one, I ran over to the back of their formation— and the sergeant leading them yelled at me.

"Chandler! Where were you?"

"Sorry, Sergeant, I fell. I fell in the gravel back there. I'm okay now."

And the sergeant never said another word. Later that night in the barracks as we were getting ready for "lights out" some of my friends asked me, "How did you like the tower?"

And I said, "Didn't do it."

They were astonished. I told them the whole story and they laughed. I mean, really laughed a lot. I was surprised. I thought they would hate me for my cowardice, but they liked what I did!

This phenomenon has always amazed me. The more I tell people about certain shameful acts of cowardice I have done, they laugh and say they feel closer to me now. How is that?

I used to be so afraid of public speaking that I literally could not do it. I would seize up. My throat would close. I would feel such a pressure on my chest that I couldn't catch my breath to speak. When I did speak my voice was so shaky it sounded like I was talking through a window fan.

When I gave my first seminars I was so scared that I could not bear to have the people in the room looking at me. Look at their eyes! Staring at me like WHO'S HE? WHY IS HE IN FRONT OF US? WHY SHOULD WE LISTEN TO HIM? WE MIGHT SOON HATE THIS GUY!

So I would pass out little Xeroxed hand-outs. I'd pass them out front to back . . . I would start my speech as I was handing them out . . . so they were not looking at me, they were occupied with the hand-outs.

Some of them said. "Here, I have one too many in this row; are these two stuck together?" I went over and fixed that as I kept talking about my subject as I moved back, back, from the front of the room to the back. Soon I had handed the last sheets out to the back row and now I WAS IN THE BACK OF THE ROOM STILL TALKING AND ALL I SAW WAS THE BACKS OF THEIR HEADS!

I would then move slowly up the middle aisle, still talking all the way, telling them to please look at their handouts, and as I got to the front of the room I realized I was okay. My initial butterflies were gone, and they had nice expressions on their faces, and I knew I would now be able to do the course.

I had created a way to dance my fear away. What a process fear can put us through. What a dance we dance with the devil himself by the light of the moon. But then how nice to finally know . . . to see the mind shift into *knowing* that it is all just a dance. And anyone can dance. Even you. Even me.

There's a blaze of light in every word.
It doesn't matter which you heard,
the holy or the broken hallelujah.

~ Leonard Cohen

81

How did he learn to be happy?

I have no money, no resources, no hopes.
I am the happiest man alive.

~ Henry Miller

Why would you be the happiest man alive, Henry?

How could that be?

You have no money. No resources. Don't you know that people strive to amass resources so they can finally be happy? And yet you are happy without them?

You have no hopes! You are just the creative, compulsive, rapid-writing, productive and prolific Henry Miller. Clue! There's a clue in there. There's a blaze of light in every word you write.

You can tell from reading his quote above and other ebullient writings from the ecstatic Henry Miller that he had experienced some glorious mind shifting early in his life. You could tell it shifted his world. And because of that, ordinary circumstances held no negative power over him. He wrote about them and made them poetic.

Most people aren't there yet.

But any mind can shift like his.

I once thought that mind shifting would be the ultimate

success course. Once I taught my attendees the things I've put in this book, they would be breaking free! But the very phrase "success course" implies lots of learning and lots of information.

I finally saw that mind shifting is not like that. It's a different kind of course. Rather than a course of study, it's more like the way a river "courses." That's the kind of course it really is. A river courses through the woodlands into the valley. The clear water courses through the land, and runs to the sea, building momentum all the way. All by itself. Without my controlling it, or trying to grasp it.

I can just step back and celebrate it.

And I can hardly speak,
my heart is beating so . . .

~ Ray Charles
"You Don't Know Me"

About the author

Steve Chandler has written dozens of books on subjects that swing dizzyingly from Jane Austen to baseball to business coaching to travel to obituaries to Moby Dick. He is the author of the bestsellers *Crazy Good* and *Time Warrior*.

He lives in Birmingham, Michigan, with his wife and editor, Kathy, and two hell hounds.

You may find him and learn of his latest adventures at:

www.stevechandler.com.

Books by Steve Chandler

Shift Your Mind Shift The World (Revised Edition)
RIGHT NOW
Death Wish
Crazy Good
37 Ways to BOOST Your Coaching Practice
Wealth Warrior
Time Warrior
The Life Coaching Connection
Fearless
The Woman Who Attracted Money
17 Lies That Are Holding You Back
10 Commitments to Your Success
Reinventing Yourself
The Story of You
100 Ways to Motivate Yourself
How to Get Clients
50 Ways to Create Great Relationships
The Joy of Selling
Powerful Graceful Success
RelationShift (with Michael Bassoff)
The Small Business Millionaire (with Sam Beckford)
100 Ways to Create Wealth (with Sam Beckford)
9 Lies That Are Holding Your Business Back
(with Sam Beckford)
Business Coaching (with Sam Beckford)
100 Ways to Motivate Others (with Scott Richardson)
The Hands Off Manager (with Duane Black)
Two Guys On the Road (with Terrence Hill)
Two Guys Read the Box Scores (with Terrence Hill)
Two Guys Read Jane Austen (with Terrence Hill)
Two Guys Read Moby Dick (with Terrence Hill)
Two Guys Read the Obituaries (with Terrence Hill)
The Prosperous Coach (with Rich Litvin)

Audio by Steve Chandler

9 Lies That Are Holding Your Business Back
10 Habits of Successful Salespeople
17 Sales Lies
37 Ways to BOOST Your Coaching Practice (audiobook)
Are You A Doer Or A Feeler?
Challenges
Choosing
Crazy Good (audiobook)
Creating Clients: Referrals
Creating Clients: The 18 Disciplines
Creative Relationships
Death Wish (audiobook)
Expectation vs. Agreement
Fearless (audiobook)
Financially Fearless
How To Double Your Income As A Coach
How to Get Clients (audiobook)
How To Help A Pessimist
How To Solve Problems
Information vs. Transformation
Is It A Dream Or A Project?
Making A Difference
MindShift: The Steve Chandler Success Course
Ownership And Leadership
People People
Personality Reinvented
Purpose vs. Personality
Serving vs. Pleasing People
Shift Your Mind Shift The World (audiobook)
Testing vs. Trusting
The Creating Wealth audio series
The Fearless Mindset
The Focused Leader
The Function Of Optimism
The Joy Of Succeeding

The Owner / Victim Choice
The Prosperous Coach (audiobook)
The Ultimate Time Management System
Time Warrior (audiobook)
Wealth Warrior (audiobook)
Welcoming Every Circumstance
Who You Know vs. What You Do
Why Should I Reinvent Myself?
You'll Get What You Want By Asking For It

Publisher's Catalogue

The Prosperous Series

#1 The Prosperous Coach: Increase Income and Impact for You and Your Clients (Steve Chandler and Rich Litvin)

#2 The Prosperous Hip Hop Producer: My Beat-Making Journey from My Grandma's Patio to a Six-Figure Business (Curtiss King)

* * *

Devon Bandison

Fatherhood Is Leadership: Your Playbook for Success, Self-Leadership, and a Richer Life

Sir Fairfax L. Cartwright

The Mystic Rose from the Garden of the King

Steve Chandler

37 Ways to BOOST Your Coaching Practice: PLUS: the 17 Lies That Hold Coaches Back and the Truth That Sets Them Free

50 Ways to Create Great Relationships

Business Coaching (Steve Chandler and Sam Beckford)

Crazy Good: A Book of CHOICES

Death Wish: The Path through Addiction to a Glorious Life

Fearless: Creating the Courage to Change the Things You Can

RIGHT NOW: Mastering the Beauty of the Present Moment

The Prosperous Coach: Increase Income and Impact for You and Your Clients (The Prosperous Series #1) (Steve Chandler and Rich Litvin)

Shift Your Mind Shift The World (Revised Edition)

Time Warrior: How to defeat procrastination, people-pleasing, self-doubt, over-commitment, broken promises and chaos

Wealth Warrior: The Personal Prosperity Revolution

Kazimierz Dąbrowski

Positive Disintegration

The Philosophy of Essence: A Developmental Philosophy Based on the Theory of Positive Disintegration

Charles Dickens

A Christmas Carol: A Special Full-Color, Fully-Illustrated Edition

James F. Gesualdi

Excellence Beyond Compliance: Enhancing Animal Welfare Through the Constructive Use of the Animal Welfare Act

Janice Goldman

Let's Talk About Money: The Girlfriends' Guide to Protecting Her ASSets

Sylvia Hall

This Is Real Life: Love Notes to Wake You Up

Christy Harden

Guided by Your Own Stars: Connect with the Inner Voice and Discover Your Dreams

I Heart Raw: Reconnection and Rejuvenation Through the Transformative Power of Raw Foods

Curtiss King

The Prosperous Hip Hop Producer: My Beat-Making Journey from My Grandma's Patio to a Six-Figure Business (The Prosperous Series #2)

David Lindsay

A Blade for Sale: The Adventures of Monsieur de Mailly

Abraham H. Maslow

The Psychology of Science: A Reconnaissance

Being Abraham Maslow (DVD)

Maslow and Self-Actualization (DVD)

Albert Schweitzer

Reverence for Life: The Words of Albert Schweitzer

William Tillier

Personality Development Through Positive Disintegration: The Work of Kazimierz Dąbrowski

Margery Williams

The Velveteen Rabbit: or How Toys Become Real

Colin Wilson

New Pathways in Psychology: Maslow and the Post-Freudian Revolution

Join our Mailing List:

www.MauriceBassett.com

MAURICE BASSETT

books for athletes of the mind